WRITING DOWN THE DAYS

365
Creative Journaling Ideas
For Young People

Lorraine M. Dahlstrom

Edited by Pamela Espeland

Free Spirit®
PUBLISHING

Library of Congress Cataloging-in-Publication Data

Dahlstrom, Lorraine M.
  Writing down the days: 365 creative journaling ideas for young people / Lorraine M. Dahlstrom; edited by Pamela Espeland.
    p. cm.
  Summary: Presents journal-writing assignments for each day of the year.
    ISBN 0-915793-19-9
    1. English language — Composition and exercises. 2. Diaries — Authorship. 3. Creative writing. [1. English language — Composition and exercises. 2. Diaries — Authorship. 3. Creative writing.] I. Espeland, Pamela, 1951– . II. Title.
PE1408.D126 1990
808'.042—dc20   89–29616
                                                                      CIP
                                                                       AC

10 9 8 7 6 5

Printed in the United States of America

Cover and book design by MacLean & Tuminelly
Cover illustration by Lisa Wagner

Dear Teacher: We hope that you will enjoy using *Writing Down the Days* in your classroom. We ask that you *not* photocopy the entries and assignments to give to your students. As teachers and former teachers, we understand that your budget for classroom materials may be tight. As publishers and authors, we ask you to respect our rights. We're working hard to bring you the best possible books at the best possible prices. If you plan to make *Writing Down the Days* part of your curriculum, call us at 1-800-735-READ and ask about our quantity discounts for teachers. We want to help!

Free Spirit Publishing Inc.
400 First Avenue North, Suite 616
Minneapolis, MN 55401
(612) 338-2068

DEDICATION

To my students, past and present, who have written volumes of journals for me and themselves;

To Lori and Marci, for their mindful support of my goals;

To Sarah, Marie, and Bill, my friends and mentors;

To David, Joel, and Jay, my masterpieces;

And to Michael, a very special person, who consistently and caringly encourages my development and growth through his own.

ABOUT THE AUTHOR

Lorraine M. Dahlstrom is a graduate of Delta College and Saginaw Valley State College at University Center, Michigan. She holds a Master's Degree in Learning and Human Development from the College of St. Thomas in St. Paul, Minnesota. She has been a secondary English teacher for more than 15 years.

Her experience includes teaching English and Language Arts at the secondary level for the Rosemount, Minnesota School District #196, and in the alternative learning program, Project ReEntry, for the Bloomington, Minnesota Public School District #272. She has been an Enhanced Learning Program Coordinator and has served on various curriculum writing projects.

Lorraine enjoys reading, weaving, and teaching traditional handcrafts in Adult Community Education classes. Currently she is writing children's books. She is the mother of three sons.

CONTENTS

ACKNOWLEDGMENTS

Many people supported and encouraged me through this, my first book. Thanks especially to Judy Galbraith, Free Spirit president and publisher, for having faith in my proposal. Thanks to Pamela Espeland, my editor, for pep talks, phone calls, and stern reminders to "just get it done!" Thanks to the Augsburg Park Library staff for enduring endless pesky questions. Thanks to my teaching team partners Ann Devine and Cindy Howard — you know what you did for me. And thanks to Dick Barnes for being my boss.

I especially want to acknowledge Nancy Pollette and Thea Holton, whose seminars on teaching techniques reinforced the processes I use in my own classroom. They also pointed me toward valuable resources, many of which I consulted in preparing this book. If you should ever hear that Nancy Pollette and Thea Holton are offering a workshop in your area, don't miss it.

INTRODUCTION

TO TEACHERS

"Write about what you did over summer vacation..."

How many years have you given that assignment? As a teacher, aren't you tired of reading about vacations? And don't you think your students are tired of *writing* about them?

This book gives you 365 chances to try something different, plus one more for Leap Year. Each assignment is unique. No two are alike. All are tied to the calendar year. All are designed to help you learn more about your students, for the more you know about them, the better you will be able to deal with them as individuals.

Often, as you're watching TV or listening to the radio, you may hear something like, "On this day in 1962..." It's fun to find out what happened in the past. At least, I always thought it was fun, and out of my enjoyment grew *Writing Down the Days*. I began investigating what had happened on certain days throughout the year, and I started basing writing assignments for my students on the information I gathered. I was amazed at how much more they wrote and how much more interesting their writing became.

Even reluctant writers have had great success using this material. Students have learned much about themselves through thoughtful consideration of the topics. I have heard students telling their friends, outside of my classroom, what the topic for the day was, and discussing it in the halls after class.

The intent of this book is to provide an outlet for private, ungraded, uncensored expression of your students' thoughts, imagination, and feelings. If it is incorporated into the curriculum — if journaling becomes a regular, accepted part of what your students do each day in school — the finished product will be a chronological document detailing a personal year. At least three important objectives will have been accomplished (and probably more):

1. First, your students will be better writers. That is practically unavoidable and virtually guaranteed!

2. Second, some of your students may have begun a journaling habit that will sustain them for the rest of their lives, thanks to you.

3. Third, all of your students will have something to look back on later in life, a glimpse

1

into their own past with insights into how they have matured and changed. They will know themselves better as a result. Don't you wish you had kept a journal starting in grade school and continuing through today? (It's not too late to start.)

Since I have used much of this information for many years in my own classrooms, with students ranging in age from seventh graders to twenty-year-old, high-school dropouts, I offer the following proven suggestions.

How to use this book

• If possible, give each student a copy of *Writing Down the Days* to use throughout the year — just like a reading, math, or history textbook. If this isn't possible, post each day's assignment somewhere in the classroom. Students may begin the assignment on their own when they enter the classroom, while you take care of attendance matters and make-up notices.

• Your students will need something to write in. A spiral binder is the most obvious choice. A stenographer's notebook, which provides a writing space of a different shape, has been very successful with my students. A three-pronged folder, in which each new entry is placed at the back, also works well.

Students may cover their folders with collages of words and pictures representing current interests, feelings, ambitions, or whatever else they choose. The collages themselves become ways to learn more about your students. When a student's folder is completely covered, use clear contact paper to protect the collage.

• Students should write a minimum of one paragraph for each assignment. In my classroom, a paragraph consists of no fewer than three sentences. Some students require the structure of minimums. Don't limit *how much* they can write; do limit *how little*. Be firm and you'll probably see paragraphs getting longer instead of shorter.

• Encourage students to leave ample space between entries. They should be able to return to specific entries later to add information. (Generous spacing also makes for easier reading.)

• Each assignment should be dated. This eliminates confusion and offers a look at how the individual student's writing has improved. You may even ask students to reproduce particular entries for more formal grading.

• Once a week or so, give students extra time to look back and read earlier entries. They can make corrections, if necessary, or expand an entry with new thoughts or information they have since learned.

- You may want to discuss some topics with your students before they begin writing. Let them know how you would answer some of the questions. Students enjoy learning about their teachers, too.

- Many assignments include addresses where students can write to find out more. You can make this step part of an assignment, or let students choose to do it or not. A stamped, self-addressed, business-size envelope should accompany each request for information.

Grading student assignments

- How you choose to do this will, of course, depend on your personal grading system. From my experience, I recommend that you use a plus for a job well done, a checkmark for an adequate job, and a minus when additional effort is called for. Try to avoid letter grades. Whatever you decide, be sure to inform your students ahead of time as to how you will be grading or keeping track of their work.

- When grading a student journal, write your comments and reactions on a separate note, then slip it inside. Don't write directly on a student's materials.

- Give extra credit when a student receives a response to a request for more informa-

tion. (A response indicates that the request letter was written appropriately.)

Going beyond the book

- I encourage you to read ahead in the assignments. Try to connect writing assignments to classroom projects or study topics. This will make them more meaningful, and students will be able to bring knowledge gained in the classroom to their writing assignments.

- Give your students opportunities to find out more about specific days. Assign research projects using library materials. Bring current newspapers, news magazines, and other resources into class for students to page through and read.

- Should a student have difficulty writing on a specific topic, be flexible. The point is not to "write to order," but simply to *write*. Offer alternative suggestions of your own; encourage your student to come up with ideas.

Privacy and storage

- A student's writing should remain private between the student and you. Parents should be shown a student's journal *only* with his or her permission.

There are rare exceptions to this rule. If a student's journal entries indicate the presence of serious problems at home or in the student's personal life, consult the school counselor or other appropriate authorities. Use your own best judgment in matters like these. If a student entry looks like a cry for help, don't ignore it.

• Store student journals in the classroom on a permanent basis. For example, you could designate a special basket as the "journals basket," or use a special box or a drawer in a file cabinet.

• I don't recommend letting students take their journals home in between assignments. It's too easy to lose or misplace all that valuable work! Instead, hand them out at the end of the year.

Finally...

Many of the celebrations, birthdays, holidays, anniversaries, commemorations, and other important dates mentioned in *Writing Down the Days* are described in *Chase's Annual Events, Special Days, Weeks and Months*. This book is updated annually and would make a valuable resource for your classroom. For more information, write to or call:

Contemporary Books
Dept. C.
180 North Michigan Avenue
Chicago, IL 60601
Telephone: (312) 782-9181

Dates given and events described are as accurate as possible. Because of the Julian calendar being transposed into the Gregorian calendar (an excellent research topic in its own right), there were sometimes slight discrepancies in the research materials I used. In general, I opted for the date most commonly found, or I added a statement or two explaining that the event described occurs near (if not on) a given date. For more precise information, consult the current *Chase's*.

I am sure you will think of many more creative and interesting ways to use this book. Write and tell me the ones that work best for you. You may write to me at the following address:

Lorraine Dahlstrom
c/o Free Spirit Publishing, Inc.
400 First Avenue North,
Suite 616
Minneapolis, MN 55401

I learned a great deal doing the research for this book. I hope you and your students gain some personal insight and knowledge from it, too.

TO PARENTS

With television, video games, and various types of audio equipment, young people today are stimulated from all sides. Teachers need help fighting the competition.

How often have you encouraged your children to write a letter to Aunt Sarah, or a thank-you note to grandparents, or a postcard to a faraway friend? How often have they done it? Kids should be encouraged to write more. In fact, they should be required to write more, and not just at school. If you insist on this with your children, you will be providing them with the means to grow in many areas of their lives.

If you have bought *Writing Down the Days* to use at home, congratulations! If you have learned that your children are using this book in school, you have a perfect opportunity to support and enhance their school work. It's not at all difficult to find writing topics around the house. Here's a list of suggestions to get you started:

• A creative grocery list

• A detailed description of one's whereabouts for a refrigerator note

• More complete phone messages

• "Reviews" of favorite television shows

• Short stories to be read to younger brothers and sisters

Add your own ideas to this list. Try them out on your children. Ask them to contribute their own suggestions. And make ample supplies available: paper, envelopes, stamps, pens and pencils. Writing letters is more fun when kids are encouraged to decorate them with drawings, cut-outs, rubber stamps, or whatever you have on hand.

Parenting is such a difficult job, and we all have such busy lives, that parents spend relatively little time communicating with their children about pleasant things. Consider keeping an *interactive journal* with your daughter or son. Choose a colored folder or stenographer's notebook to contain your correspondence. Each day, share some good news, a compliment, a funny story, or a fond memory. Make this something special, just between the two of you. If you have more than one child who wants to participate in this special activity, let each select a different colored paper or ink. Keep individual children's entries private. This type of journaling gives you a direct line of communication to and from your child.

Help your children find the time to write. Set aside a quiet place for thinking and writing. Provide lots of encouragement. I promise that you'll see a difference — in your child's school work and self-esteem, and in your relationship with your child.

TO YOUNG WRITERS

Express yourself! That's what this book is for. It is meant to help you express your own creativity through writing.

Maybe you think that writing is boring. You're tired of writing about the same old stuff. This book should change your mind.

For one thing, the entries are *not* boring. They are not the kinds of things you normally get to write about, especially in school. *Writing Down the Days* gives you the chance to write about your favorite pop singer...good reasons to take a day off school...your favorite stuffed animal from childhood... four wishes... your "schnozzola" (that's your NOSE!)... five things you'd tell a President... whose face you would add to Mt. Rushmore and why... something you "hate"... something silly... the scariest movie you ever saw... your "dream house"... your sneakers... and much, much more.

There's something else you should know about *Writing Down the Days*. There are no right or wrong answers to any of the exercises. You can write *your own* answers and tell *your own* ideas. You can make choices, experiment, and use your imagination. You can base what you write on your own feelings and experiences. This book is for you. Write your entries to please yourself.

Remember that you think differently from everyone else. The way you respond to each entry will be different from the way anyone else responds.

Communicate! You have things to say, and you want to say them. Use this book to help you write about things that interest you. Write about happenings and situations that have something to do with your life. Take each journal idea personally. Writing doesn't have to be boring, or hard, or painful. The more of yourself you put into it, the more you will get out of it.

You'll notice that many entries include addresses. These are real places you can write to if you want to know more about a given topic. Try it! Especially if you like to get mail. Be sure to include a self-addressed, stamped, business-size envelope with each request for information.

When you finish *Writing Down the Days*, you'll have a detailed journal of a year from your life. Put it away for a while. When you rediscover it, enjoy! You'll get to look back at your past, at the way you used to be, at the things you used to think and feel. You'll learn a lot about how you have grown and changed. It's exciting to read your own history.

Meanwhile, have fun writing down your days. Who knows

— you may decide to keep journaling for the rest of your life! Many people do. Ask your teacher or your school librarian to find some examples of people who have written journals for years and years and years. Some journals have even been published. Maybe you can read someone else's journal.

I want to know *your* opinion of *Writing Down the Days.* What do you like about it? What don't you like about it? What's your favorite entry — and your least favorite one? Is there anything you would change about the book? To give me your opinion, you'll have to WRITE me a letter. Here is where you can send it:

Lorraine Dahlstrom
c/o Free Spirit Publishing, Inc.
400 First Avenue North
Suite 616
Minneapolis, MN 55401

I hope to hear from you someday. Happy writing!

Lorraine M. Dahlstrom

WRITING DOWN THE DAYS

JANUARY 1

Happy New Year! Today is New Year's Day. It is a legal holiday in Canada and the United States. Approximately 123 other nations in the world also consider it a holiday.

Many people make New Year's Resolutions. Resolutions are decisions to do or achieve certain things. They usually involve making personal changes. For example, you might decide to make your bed every morning, to help more around the house, or to get all your things ready the night before you need them (like your clothes, or the things you need for school).

✎ **Write at least three resolutions you will make for this year. If you can't think of three things you need to work on, then make up three resolutions for someone else. Explain why you made these resolutions for yourself (or the other person).**

JANUARY 2

This is the birthday of Isaac Asimov. He was born in Russia in 1920. He came to the United States at age three and became a U.S. citizen in 1928. He received his Ph.D. from Columbia University in 1948. Asimov is a very prolific writer (meaning that he writes a lot). He has written dozens of books, articles, and short stories. Plus he has edited many collections of fantasy and science fiction. You may know him as the writer of more than 30 titles in the *How Did We Find Out...* series.

✎ **Asimov really likes to write. He likes it so much that he does it every day. Write about something you like to do so much that you'd be willing to do it every day. Tell why you like this activity, how long you've liked it, and describe any special materials or things you need to do it.**

JANUARY 3

On this day in 1959, Alaska was admitted to the United States as the 49th state. It is the largest state in terms of area, but it has a very small population. In 1867, the U.S. bought Alaska from Russia for $7.2 million dollars. In the

1890s, gold was discovered there. Many people went to Alaska in the hope of finding their fortunes. In 1968, extensive oil discoveries were made. And in 1980, huge offshore oil deposits were found.

✏️ **On March 24, 1989, the Exxon oil tanker *Valdez* ran aground in Alaska's Prince William Sound. The major oil spill that occurred made news all over the world. What was your reaction to the oil spill? Give your views on the damage and clean-up.**

JANUARY 4

Sir Isaac Newton was born on this day in 1643. He was a physicist and a mathematician. Newton is credited with the discovery of the law of gravity and became a leader in the 17th century scientific revolution. He died on March 31, 1727.

✏️ **Many people believe that Sir Isaac Newton spent a lot of time daydreaming under a local apple tree. Write about your favorite place to daydream and what you daydream about.**

JANUARY 5

This is National Hobby Month. January was named National Hobby Month to urge people to enjoy the fun and creativity of putting together models, creating crafts, and collecting collectibles. If you would like a list of hobby project directions, write to:

Hobby Industries of America
Director of Communications
319 E. 54th Street
Elmwood Park, New Jersey
07407

✏️ **Do you have a hobby? Everyone should have at least one special activity that he or she likes to do in spare time. It can be playing a game or sport, collecting certain objects, making something, or practicing one of the arts like dancing or painting. If you have a hobby, write a paragraph describing it. If you don't have a hobby, think about one you might enjoy doing. Write a paragraph about how you plan to get started on it.**

JANUARY 6

Today is the "birthday" of Sherlock Holmes. Holmes is a fictional British detective, so he wasn't really "born." He was created by a writer named Sir Arthur Conan Doyle.

Holmes is known for his powers of deduction — the ability to reach conclusions by logical reasoning. He is famous for solving unusual mysteries. He often works with a partner named Dr. Watson.

✎ **Write about a mystery you helped to solve. Maybe it was "The Mystery of the Missing Car Keys." Or "The Mystery of Who Ate the Last Piece of Cake." Tell how you used your reasoning powers to find the answer. Then describe what happened when you told the answer.**

JANUARY 7

Leddat, the official Ethiopian Christmas, takes place on January 7. There is an Ethiopian Christmas story that has been handed down for generations: When the shepherds heard of the birth of Jesus, the story goes, they were so happy that they turned over their shepherd's staffs and started to play a game. The game, a variation of field hockey, was called ganna. In Ethiopia today, Leddat is often called Ganna, and playing the game is part of the Leddat celebration.

✎ **What is your favorite winter sport — one you play, not just watch? Do you play it outdoors or indoors? Write about the sport, including the rules. If there isn't a particular winter sport you like, then write about what you do in your winter spare time.**

JANUARY 8

Elvis Presley was born on this day in 1935 in Tupelo, Mississippi. Elvis was a very popular American singer. He sang such songs as "Love Me Tender," "Hound Dog," and "Heartbreak Hotel."

✎ **Who are the most popular singers or groups today? Give their names, describe any distinctive clothing they wear, and list some of their song titles.**

JANUARY 9

On this day in 1859, Carrie Lane Chapman Catt was born in Ripon, Wisconsin. She was an American women's rights leader who founded the National League of Women Voters in 1919. She played an important role in the adoption of the Nineteenth Amendment to the United States Constitution, which gave women the right to vote. She died on March 9, 1947.

✎ **Will you vote in elections when you are old enough? Why or why not? What is so important about voting?**

JANUARY 10

On January 10, 1920, the League of Nations was founded. Fifty nations entered into a worldwide movement toward peace and cooperation. However, the League of Nations was not successful. It was dissolved on April 18, 1946.

By then the United Nations had been formed. Three months earlier, on the 26th anniversary of the founding of the League of Nations, delegates from 51 nations met in London for the first session of the UN General Assembly.

✎ **Write about what you can do to promote world peace. What can you do now? What will you be able to do when you're an adult?**

JANUARY 11

Today marks the birthday of Eugenio Maria de Hostos. He was born in Rio Canas, Puerto Rico in 1839. As a philosopher and a patriot, he brought many improvements to Latin America. He wrote over 50 books, mostly on law and education, which brought about important reforms. He was responsible for the first railroad across the Andes Mountains, which separate Chile and Argentina. He died in Santo Domingo, Dominican Republic on August 11, 1903.

✎ **Eugenio Maria de Hostos believed that you should do your best at everything you try. Do you agree? Why or why not?**

JANUARY 12

Charles Perrault was born in France on this day in 1628. During his lifetime he worked as a lawyer, a poet, and a supervisor of royal buildings for King Louis XIV. He also wrote fairy tales to amuse his children and friends. His most famous book, published in 1679, is called *Tales of Mother Goose*. You probably know many stories from this book — like "Sleeping Beauty," "Little Red Riding Hood," "Cinderella," and "Puss 'n' Boots."

✏️ **Pick a character from one of Perrault's stories and tell the story again as though you were that character.**

JANUARY 13

This is Saint Knute's Day in Sweden. Nine centuries ago, King Knute — also known as King Knut and King Canute — said that the Christmas season should last 20 days, from Christmas Day to January 13. Today Swedes have what is called Julgransplundring, or "Plundertime." They take down the Christmas tree and celebrate by dancing and eating cookie ornaments. A similar celebration, Tyvendedags Jul, marks the official end of Yuletide in Norway.

✏️ **How does your family celebrate the end of a holiday season? Which holiday is the biggest, most important, and most fun around your house?**

JANUARY 14

Today marks the Feast of Saint Sava, a children's festival held in Serbia, to honor Saint Sava. Saint Sava built schools and monasteries all over Serbia. He died on January 14, 1237. During his festival there is feasting, music, and dancing in the schools and communities.

✏️ **Students are always looking for a reason to take a day off school, and a celebration is a great reason. Describe a celebration that you would invent as a reason for getting out of school.**

JANUARY 15

Martin Luther King, Jr. was born on this day in 1929. Dr. King was a civil rights leader, a minister, and an author. He received the Nobel Peace Prize in 1964.

In 1955–56, he led a boycott of Montgomery, Alabama's segregated buses; within a year, the buses were integrated. In 1957 he organized the Southern Christian Leadership Conference to promote civil rights. He made many speeches during his lifetime, including the famous "I Have A Dream" speech.

Dr. King was assassinated in Memphis, Tennessee on April 4, 1968 at the age of 39. Now his birthday is a national holiday. It is celebrated on the third Monday in January.

✎ **Dr. King worked for peace through nonviolent means. What are your views on violence? Do you think that violence is always wrong? Or do you think there are times when violence is necessary or right? Be specific.**

JANUARY 16

Today is National Nothing Day. National Nothing Day was the idea of Harold Pullman Coffin, a newspaperman who first observed it in 1973. The reason for it, Coffin explained, was "to provide Americans with one national day when they can just sit without celebrating, observing or honoring anything." Coffin died in Capitola, California on September 12, 1981. He was 76 years old.

✎ **What is your favorite thing to do when you have the opportunity to do "nothing"? Where do you do "nothing"? And what happens when you do "nothing"?**

JANUARY 17

Benjamin Franklin was born on this day in 1706. He was the oldest person to sign both the Declaration of Independence and the Constitution. He was a scientist, printer, statesmen, inventor, diplomat, publisher, philosopher, and philanthropist. He organized a fire and police department, a postal service, a library, a hospital, and an antislavery society. The rocking chair, bifocals, and the harmonica are among his inventions. He was the author of *Poor Richard's Almanac*, which was published between 1733 and 1758. Many of the sayings in the almanac are still remembered today. Franklin died on April 17, 1790.

✎ **One of the sayings from *Poor Richard's Almanac* goes, "A stitch in time saves nine." What do you think this means? Write about ways it might apply to things other than sewing.**

JANUARY 18

Today is the birthday of Alan Alexander Milne. A. A. Milne was born in London in 1882. His son, Christopher Robin, received a toy bear for his first birthday in 1921. Over the years, Christopher Robin was given more stuffed animals, and A. A. Milne's wife, Dorothy, invented personalities for them. There was Winnie the Pooh, Eeyore, Piglet, Tigger, Kanga, and others.

You probably know these characters from the books A. A. Milne wrote about them — *Winnie the Pooh* and *The House at Pooh Corner*. He died in Hartfield, England on January 31, 1956.

✎ **Describe your favorite childhood stuffed animal. If you didn't have a stuffed animal, what was your favorite childhood toy?**

JANUARY 19

Edgar Allan Poe was born on this day in 1809. Poe was an American poet and short-story writer. He is famous for his tales of mystery and suspense. Maybe you have read or heard about "The Fall of the House of Usher," "The Murders in the Rue Morgue," and "The Pit and the Pendulum." Poe died in Baltimore, Maryland on October 7, 1849, after a very troubled life.

✎ **Write about a mystery story you remember reading, watching on TV, or seeing at the movies. Were you able to figure out the mystery before the ending? How?**

JANUARY 20

Today marks Babin Den, or Grandmother's Day in Bulgaria. It dates back to a time when women who helped to deliver babies were called baba, meaning "grandmother." It was believed that a baba passed some of her knowledge to the children she helped to deliver. Today Bulgarians remember this day with traditional celebrations and festivities.

✎ **Write about your grandmother. If you don't have a grandmother, write about what the ideal grandma would be like.**

JANUARY 21

John Charles Fremont, nicknamed "The Pathfinder," was an American surveyor and army officer famous for leading expeditions to explore the early West. He was born on January 21, 1813.

Thomas Jonathan Jackson, nicknamed "Stonewall" Jackson, was a Confederate General in the Civil War. It is said that he was called "Stonewall" because of his bravery in battle. He was born on January 21, 1824.

✎ **Many people know only the nicknames of these men and not their full names. Someone's nickname might describe his or her size, beliefs, likes or dislikes, or something he or she has accomplished. Or it may be just a shorter version of a long name. Do you have a nickname? If you do, what is it? Who calls you by your nickname? Does it have a special meaning? If you don't have a nickname, write about someone who does. Or write about a nickname you'd like to have and why.**

JANUARY 22

Today is National Popcorn Day. Popcorn is a must at a movie. Many people fix microwave popcorn to eat at home. You can even buy already-popped popcorn in many different flavors, from Sour Cream and Onion to Cheddar Cheese. "Air popped" popcorn has no salt or butter and is a good snack for calorie watchers. If you would like more information about popcorn, write to:

The Popcorn Institute
111 E. Wacker Drive, Suite 600
Chicago, Illinois 60601

✎ **What is your favorite kind of popcorn? Where do you usually eat it? Is there someone you usually eat it with? If you don't like popcorn, write about another favorite snack.**

JANUARY 23

This is National Handwriting Day. It is also the birthday of John Hancock, who was an American patriot and statesman. Hancock was the first signer of the Declaration of Independence. He wrote his signature in very large letters to make sure that King George would be able to read it without wearing his glasses. His name now refers to anyone's handwritten signature. When you sign something, you are putting your "John Hancock" on it.

✎ **Write a paragraph in your best handwriting. It can be on any topic you choose. Just be sure to put your "John Hancock" at the end.**

JANUARY 24

Today begins the Alacitas Fair, an annual three-day celebration held by the Aymara Indians of Bolivia. The Alacitas Fair has been held at La Paz for hundreds of years to honor Ekeko, the Aymaras' god of prosperity.

Ekeko is pictured as a little man with a big belly, an open mouth, and arms spread out wide. He carries an empty pack on his back. During the fair, the Aymaras carry statues and dolls of Ekeko. They put miniature replicas of food, clothing, and other items they would like to have in Ekeko's pack. They believe that if they do this, the god will bring them the real things.

✎ **What things would you put in Ekeko's pack if you went to the Alacitas Fair? List at least four things you would like to have.**

JANUARY 25

Today is Burns Day, a special day in Scotland, England, and Newfoundland. It commemorates the birth on January 25, 1759 of Robert Burns, Scotland's most famous poet. He was born in Ayrshire, Scotland and died at Dumfries on July 21, 1796.

When Burns Day draws to a close, celebrants sing "Auld Lang Syne," which Burns wrote as a tribute to friendship. Burns also wrote, "Oh wad some power the giftie gie us/To see oursels as others see us!" A rough translation of this might go: "If only some power would give us the gift/To see ourselves the way others see us!"

✏️ **How do others see you? If a person did not know you, what could he or she find out about you from the way you act, the way you talk, the way you dress, the way you treat other people?**

JANUARY 26

Foundation Day, or Australia Day, is a public holiday in Australia to honor the landing of Captain Arthur Phillip on the Australian continent in 1788. It is celebrated on January 26, if that day is a Monday, or on the first Monday after the 26th. Foundation Day has been observed every year since 1817.

When Captain Phillip came to Australia, his ship was full of convicts sent there to relieve the overcrowded British prisons. Some of the prisoners had volunteered to go to Australia because the prisons in England were so terrible.

✏️ **Which do you think would be better? To stay in an overcrowded prison close to home, or to travel a long distance to an unknown land where you would not be in a crowded prison, but instead in a penal colony or settlement? Tell why you would make that choice.**

JANUARY 27

Today is the birthday of Charles Lutwidge Dodgson. He was an English mathematician, author, and portrait photographer. He became a deacon of Christ Church, but he never became a priest because he stammered. He most enjoyed preaching to children. One of his favorite listeners was a young girl named Alice Liddell, the daughter of the Dean of Christ Church. In July of 1862, Dodgson began telling Alice and her sisters about "Alice's adventures underground." He wrote out the story as a gift for Alice in Christmas of 1864. In 1865, he published *Alice's Adventures in Wonderland* under the name of Lewis Carroll. That book has been translated into more languages than almost any other book except the Bible.

 **"Cheshire..." said Alice, "would you tell me, please, which way I ought to go from here?"**

"That depends a good deal on where you want to get to," said the Cat.

"I don't much care where — " said Alice.

"Then it doesn't matter which way you go," said the Cat.

"— so long as I get somewhere," Alice added as an explanation.

"Oh, you're sure to do that," said the Cat, "if you only walk long enough."

Write about "somewhere" you would like to "get" — and the way you would choose to go.

JANUARY 28

This day marks the anniversary of the explosion of the space shuttle *Challenger* in 1986. At 11:39A.M. EST, the shuttle was 74 seconds into its flight and about 10 miles above the Earth when it exploded. All seven crew members were killed, the *Challenger* was destroyed, and the United States Space Program was temporarily sus-

pended. Christa McAuliffe, a teacher who was the first ordinary citizen in space, died along with astronauts Francis R. Scobee, Michael J. Smith, Judith A. Resnik, Ellison S. Onizuka, Ronald E. McNair and Gregory B. Jarvis.

The *Challenger* disaster was a terrible tragedy. However, most space flights are safe and successful. The majority of astronauts and cosmonauts have flown in space with no accidents or problems.

How old were you when the *Challenger* was lost? Do you remember what happened? Tell what you remember. How do you feel about the space shuttle program starting again? Have you ever thought about being part of the space program? If so, what would you like to do?

JANUARY 29

Today is the anniversary of the establishment of the Baseball Hall of Fame in 1936. The first five men named to the Hall of

Fame were Ty Cobb, Walter Johnson, Christy Mathewson, Honus Wagner, and Babe Ruth. Since then about 200 more men have been elected to the Hall of Fame.

✎ **Baseball has become a sport enjoyed all over the world. Which team do you support? List some of the players and give some other information about the team. If you don't follow baseball, write about another team sport you like.**

JANUARY 30

Today is the birthday of FDR. The initials FDR stand for Franklin Delano Roosevelt. Born in Hyde Park, New York, in 1882, FDR was the only U.S. President to serve more than two terms. He died in Warm Springs, Georgia while he was still in office.

FDR was a philatelist — a stamp collector. If you would like more information about stamp collecting, write to:

Junior Philatelists of America
P.O. Box 850
Boalsburg, PA 16827

✎ **What do you collect? Write about your collection. If you don't collect anything, write about something you think would be fun to collect.**

JANUARY 31

On January 31, 1947, in Whitehorse, Canada, a town in the Yukon Territory, the temperature reached 62 degrees Fahrenheit below zero. This was the coldest temperature ever recorded in Canada.

✎ **It probably never gets that cold where you live! Write about the temperatures in your area. How cold does it get? How hot does it get? What is your favorite temperature? Why?**

FEBRUARY 1

On February 1, 1709, Scottish sailor Alexander Selkirk was rescued after spending almost five years alone on a deserted island. He had asked to be left there in September, 1704, after an argument with the ship's captain. His adventures led Daniel Defoe to write *Robinson Crusoe*.

✎ **Imagine that you are going to be alone on an island for one year. You can only take five things with you. (Don't worry about food, shelter, and clothing; those things will be provided.) List the five things you would take and tell why you would take them.**

FEBRUARY 2

This is Candlemas Day, a religious festival day. In Pennsylvania there is a Candlemas Day tradition of searching for a groundhog named "Punxsutawney Phil," who is supposedly the King of the Weather Prophets. This custom dates back to earlier Candlemas Days, when people searched for European hedgehogs. Since there were no European hedgehogs in New England, the German settlers there searched for groundhogs instead.

In the United States, this day is known as Groundhog Day. The groundhog comes out of hibernation. If he sees his shadow, he retreats back into his hole for six more weeks of winter.

✎ **How can you tell when spring is almost here? Describe the "clues" you can see, smell, hear, and touch.**

FEBRUARY 3

Sestubun, the Bean-Throwing Festival, begins today in Japan. The festival celebrates the beginning of spring and the end of winter. The bean-throwing ceremony has its roots in ancient times. Throughout Japan, public ceremonies are held at temples and shrines. Celebrities throw beans to the waiting crowd. A bean that is caught is believed to bring good luck to the catcher.

✎ **Imagine that your family is hosting an exchange student from Japan. Explain a local custom that you think the student should know about. It can be a national custom or a local custom.**

FEBRUARY 4

Born on this day in Detroit, Michigan, in 1902, Charles A. Lindbergh made aviation history. In 1927 he flew alone, nonstop across the Atlantic Ocean from New York to Paris, France. This marked the first time anyone had accomplished this feat. Lindbergh became known as "the Lone Eagle" after making the 3,600 mile trip in 33½ hours to win a $25,000 prize. He had no radio or navigation equipment.

Lindbergh died on August 27, 1974.

✎ **Pretend that it is 1902 and you are giving Lindbergh last-minute instructions before his takeoff. Offer him some good advice on ways to stay awake, take care of himself, and have a safe trip.**

FEBRUARY 5

This is Weatherman's Day. It commemorates the birth of America's first weather reporter, John Jeffries.

Jeffries was a Boston doctor. He kept detailed records of weather conditions in the Boston area from 1774 to 1816 — except for the period from March 4, 1776 and May 27, 1790, when he was interrupted by the Revolutionary War. Jeffries knew Benjamin Franklin, who was also interested in the weather.

✎ **Write about what you consider to be an ideal day, as far as the weather is concerned. If you had your choice, where would you go and what would you do to enjoy this ideal day?**

FEBRUARY 6

Sapporo is a city in northern Japan. For three days, beginning today, groups of people will build huge snow sculptures in a place called Odori Park. They may use steel frames, tons of snow brought down from the mountains, and ice that has been chopped out of the river. The sculptures will be part of the Sapporo Snow Festival.

The festival had its beginnings in 1949, when some children built six huge snowmen. The snowmen were so popular that the city now sponsors a snow sculpture contest every year.

✎ **Have you ever built a snowman? If yes, write directions for building a snowman. Imagine that the person who will be reading your directions has never even seen snow before. (Your directions will have to be very clear!) Or, if you have never built a snowman, write a description of what you think it would be like to build one.**

FEBRUARY 7

Charles Dickens was born on this day in Portsmouth, England, in 1812. He was an author whose most popular works include *Oliver Twist*, *David Copperfield*, *A Tale of Two Cities*, and *A Christmas Carol*.

Dickens died at Gad's Hill, England on June 9, 1870. He is buried in Westminster Abbey.

✎ **One of Dickens's best-known characters is Scrooge in *A Christmas Carol*. For most of the story, Scrooge is a mean and stingy man. Is it ever a good idea to be stingy?**

Yes or no? When and why (or why not)?

FEBRUARY 8

Today marks the birthday of the Boy Scouts of America. Boy Scouts Day falls near this date each year, during Anniversary Week. The Boy Scouts organization was started in 1910 by a man named William Boyce. He originally had the idea when he traveled to England, got lost, and was helped by a young person.

The Boy Scouts' motto is "Be Prepared," and scouts learn while doing various things to earn merit badges. The Scouts encourage decision-making skills and physical fitness. If you would like more information about the Boy Scouts, write to:

Boy Scouts of America
1325 Walnut Hill Lane
Irving, Texas 75038-3096

✎ **One requirement for the Boy Scout merit badge for citizenship is to describe your community to a scout from another state or province. Write a description of your community. Tell about its schools, churches, ethnic makeup, businesses, and points of interest.**

FEBRUARY 9

On February 9, 1870, the United States National Weather Service was established. The Weather Service is a part of the United States Government. It is responsible for observing and forecasting the weather. Over 300 full-time weather stations collect and analyze information from the military and other agencies to come up with the most accurate weather facts and predictions possible.

✎ In 1890, Charles Dudley Warner wrote, "Everybody talks about the weather, but nobody does anything about it." Warner's observation about the weather was published in the *Courant* newspaper in Hartford, Connecticut. (Many people attribute this remark to Mark Twain.) For some people, the weather is very important to their jobs — even their lives. Write about people who must pay close attention to the weather, and tell why.

FEBRUARY 10

On this day in 1893, James Francis Durante was born in New York City. He grew up to be Jimmy Durante, American comedian, composer, actor, and author. He was famous for the hat he wore and his big nose, which he referred to as his "schnozzola." On his weekly television show, he would often sing his trademark song, "Inka Dinka Doo," and he always ended the show with, "Good Night, Mrs. Calabash, wherever you are." Jimmy Durante died on January 29, 1980.

✎ Write a paragraph about your "schnozzola." Is it too big, too small, or just right? Would you change it if you could? Why or why not?

FEBRUARY 11

National Science Youth Day is observed today, on Thomas Alva Edison's birthday, as part of National Electrical Week. Edison was born in Milan, Ohio, in 1847. During his 84 years, he created 1,097 inventions including the phonograph and the incandescent lightbulb.

✎ **Have you ever invented anything? If yes, describe your invention — what it was made of, what it was meant to do. If not, write about something you would like to invent.**

FEBRUARY 12

Abraham Lincoln was born on this day in 1809. He was the 16th President of the United States and the first to be assassinated. On Good Friday, April 14, 1865, while watching a performance of the play, *Our American Cousin*, at Ford's Theatre in Washington, D.C., he was shot by John Wilkes Booth. The President died the next day.

Lincoln's presidency encompassed the tragic Civil War. He is especially remembered for his Emancipation Proclamation, his Gettysburg Address ("Four score and seven years ago..."), and his proclamation establishing the last Thursday of November as Thanksgiving Day.

✎ **Imagine that you were in the audience at Ford's Theatre the night Lincoln was shot. Describe**

what happened, including sights, sounds, and your reactions. An encyclopedia or your history book will give you details if you are unsure of the facts.

FEBRUARY 13

On this date in 1988, LEGO Systems, Incorporated sponsored an International Building contest in Billund, Denmark. People from all over the world met to make things out of LEGO plastic building blocks. The LEGO company plans to sponsor other international contests in the future. If you would like more information on LEGOs or the contest, write to:

LEGO Systems, Incorporated
Public Relations Department
555 Taylor Road
Enfield, Connecticut 06082

✎ **Some adults have large collections of LEGOs, dolls, or trains. What "toy" do you think you might still like to have around when you are an adult? Why?**

FEBRUARY 14

Nobody seems to know the real beginnings of Valentine's Day. Some say that it was started to honor two beheaded martyrs, each supposedly named Valentine. Others say it had nothing to do with the martyrs, but was thought to be the day birds chose their mates. Still others claim that it began with Lupercalia, an ancient Roman festival.

Today Valentine's Day is the most widely observed unofficial holiday in the world. It is celebrated with gifts, cards, and candy in England, France, the United States, and other nations.

✎ **Write a Valentine's Day greeting to someone you like very much. Then write the Valentine's Day greeting you wish that person would send to you.**

FEBRUARY 15

On February 15, 1812, Charles Lewis Tiffany was born in Killingly, Connecticut. Tiffany was an American jeweler who became famous for the high-quality jewelry sold by his company, Tiffany's. He died in New York City on February 18, 1902.

✎ **Describe your favorite piece of jewelry and tell why you like it so much. Or write about a piece of jewelry you wish you had and tell why. Or, if you don't like jewelry, write about why you think jewelry isn't important.**

FEBRUARY 16

Basant Panchami, a Hindu celebration of spring, starts today. Basant is a Hindu word meaning "spring." The festival also honors Sarasvati, the Hindu goddess of learning and the arts. Students who want special help on their exams go to her temple, leaving behind gifts like pens, brushes, and books.

✎ **If you could get special help with an exam, which exam would it be? What kind of help would you ask for?**

FEBRUARY 17

Rene Theophile Laennec, a French physician, was born on February 17, 1781. He was called "The Father of Chest Medicine" because he invented the stethoscope in 1817. A stethoscope is used to listen to the heart and other organs inside the body. At first Laennec used paper tubes to make his stethoscope, and later he used hollow wooden cylinders. With his homemade stethoscopes, Laennec listened to people's body sounds. Then he wrote descriptions of what he heard. His descriptions were so detailed and so precise that other doctors used them to diagnose diseases correctly. Laennec became an expert on tuberculosis and died from it on August 13, 1826.

✎ **Write about the last time you had to visit the doctor.**

FEBRUARY 18

Solomon Rabinowitz was a Russian author who used the pen name Sholom Aleichem. He was born February 18, 1859. He was praised as a master of the short story form, and some historians called him "the Yiddish Mark Twain." Aleichem died on May 13, 1916.

✎ **Both Mark Twain and Sholom Aleichem often wrote about people and places they were very familiar with. If you were to write a short story, what characters (people you know) might you include? Write a short description of each character.**

FEBRUARY 19

An organization called the Knights of Pythias was founded on this day in 1864 in Washington, D.C. The Knights is a fraternal order — an organization for men. The Knights are named after a Greek named Pythias, one of a pair of famous friends. Here is their story.

Two men named Damon and Pythias lived in Syracuse, Greece, around the fourth century. Pythias was condemned to death for plotting against the government. Pythias asked Dionysius, the ruler of Syracuse, if he could go home to put his personal affairs in order before his death. His home was some distance away from Syracuse, but Dionysius said that Pythias could go — under one condition. If Pythias didn't come back in time, then Damon, his best friend, would die in his place!

Damon agreed to this, trusting that Pythias would return. Then Pythias was delayed on the way back to Syracuse. Damon was just about to be put to death when Pythias arrived. Dionysius was so impressed by the friendship between the two men that he let them both go. Afterward, he asked if he could be their friend, too.

✎ **Describe the "perfect best friend." Tell what that person looks like, says, and does, and how you feel when you are with that person.**

FEBRUARY 20

On February 20, 1962, the first United States astronaut orbited the Earth. John Glenn Day commemorates his launch from Cape Canaveral, Florida. Glenn circled the Earth three times in his space capsule before landing safely in the Atlantic Ocean.

✎ **This was a very courageous act. Write a paragraph or more about courage. Tell about something you have done that** you consider courageous. Or describe something courageous that someone you know has done.

FEBRUARY 21

If you had lived in New Haven, Connecticut, on this day in 1878, you might have received the very first United States telephone book ever to be printed. Only 50 names were listed in it. The first telephone exchange in the United States opened in New Haven on January 28, 1878.

✎ **Write about five ways you can use a telephone book — not including looking up telephone numbers or other printed information. (For example: Propping doors open...for little kids to sit on at the dinner table...) Be creative!**

FEBRUARY 22

On February 22, 1732, George Washington was born. His name is one of the best-known in United States history. Washington played a very important part in the American Revolution against Great Britain. When he died, General Henry Lee said that Washington had been "first in war, first in peace, and first in the hearts of his countrymen." Over the years, the former President has been given the title, "The Father of His Country."

✎ **Write five things you would like to tell the President of your choice. You may pick the current President or any President from the past or the future.**

FEBRUARY 23

Samuel Pepys (pronounced "Peeps") was born in Cambridge, England, on February 23, 1633. He was the author of one of the most famous diaries in the world. He wrote it in his own shorthand language, and it was not deciphered until 1825.

Pepys kept his Diary from January 1660 to May 31, 1669. Those years proved to be a very exciting period of English history. Pepys included many

entries on the manners, gossip, and politics of his day.

✎ **Pretend that you are Samuel Pepys, writing in his diary — only you are writing about today, not 300 years ago. Tell about current events, social customs (what people are saying, doing, and wearing), and more. Make your entry as interesting as you can!**

FEBRUARY 24

Wilhelm Carl Grimm, a German mythologist and author, was born on this day in 1786. He and his brother Jacob wrote *Grimm's Fairy Tales*.

Many of the fairy tales in their book — including "Rapunzel," "Hansel and Gretel," "Cinderella," and "Rumpelstiltskin" — had already been around for a long time. German peasants had been telling them for many, many years. But nobody had ever written them down before. By writing them down, the brothers Grimm made it possible for people all over the world to read and enjoy these old fairy tales.

In 1983, *The New York Times* reported that another tale by Wilhelm Grimm had been discovered after more than 150 years. The story, written in a letter Grimm wrote to a little girl, had never been published. If you would like to read this story, go to your library and ask for *Dear Mili*, illustrated by Maurice Sendak. (For more about Maurice Sendak, see pages 73–74, June 10 entry.)

✎ **Describe the plot of your favorite fairy tale or story. Write as if you were a newspaper or television reporter. Remember that reporters are supposed to answer these questions: "Who?" "What?" "Where?" "When?" "Why?"**

FEBRUARY 25

Enrico Caruso was born in Naples, Italy, on February 25, 1873. During his lifetime, he became the world's most famous opera singer, and many people today still consider him the greatest ever. Caruso died in 1921.

✎ **Caruso probably isn't your favorite singer. You may not even like opera. (Then again, maybe you do!) Write about your favorite singer. What kind of music does he or she sing? Which song do you like best? Write down some of the lyrics, if you know them.**

FEBRUARY 26

Jackie Gleason was born on this day in 1916 in Brooklyn, New York. His real name was Herbert John Gleason. He was an actor and a comedian, star of the long-running television series, *The Honeymooners*. In *The Honeymooners*, Gleason played a big, loud-mouthed bus driver named Ralph Kramden. Gleason died in 1987.

✎ **Write the words, "I saw something funny today...," and describe something funny that you actually saw. If you didn't see anything funny today, what about yesterday?**

FEBRUARY 27

On this day in 1807, Henry Wadsworth Longfellow was born in Portland, Maine. Longfellow was an American poet who wrote long story-telling poems. He was one of a group of New England poets who became known as the "Fireside Poets" because they had a large family audience. Families would gather around the fireside and read their poems aloud. Two of Longfellow's most famous poems are "The Children's Hour" and "The Song of Hiawatha." He died in 1882.

✎ **Write about one of the things your family does together, for fun or entertainment.**

FEBRUARY 28

On February 28, 1983, the final original *M*A*S*H* program was shown on television. M*A*S*H stands for "Mobile Army Surgical Hospital." The television series was about a fictional mobile hospital unit during the Korean War, a war that began in June 1950 and lasted three years. The television program lasted longer than the actual war — from September 17, 1972, until this day in 1983, a total of 11 years. Reruns are still shown today.

✎ **What are the television-watching rules at your house? Did your parents make them up, or did the whole family decide? If you don't have any rules about TV at your house, why do you suppose some people do?**

FEBRUARY 29

This is Leap Year Day. It has been a controversial day since the year 45 B.C., when the Roman emperor Julius Caesar decided that a year would be exactly 365 days and 6 hours long. In fact, the Earth takes 365 days, 5 hours, 45 minutes, and a little over 45 seconds to revolve around the sun.

In A.D. 1288, an Act of the Scottish Parliament said that during a Leap Year, women could propose marriage to men. Laws later passed in France and Italy said much the same thing. That is why, in some parts of the world, today is called Bachelors' Day.

✎ **What would you do if your birthday fell on February 29? When and how would you celebrate it during non-Leap Years? How would you keep track of your age? If your birthday really does fall on February 29, write about what it's like to have a Leap Year birthday.**

MARCH 1

This is the birthday of the Peace Corps. President John F. Kennedy signed an executive order to establish the Peace Corps in 1961. Since then, more that 150,000 volunteers have been sent to 94 countries. The volunteers assist the developing nations with many projects such as water sanitation, agriculture, and nutrition. If you would like more information about the Peace Corps, write to:

Peace Corps
Director of Public Affairs
Washington, D.C. 20526

✎ **If you were to volunteer for the Peace Corps today, what skill could you teach to people in a foreign country? How would learning that skill benefit the people?**

MARCH 2

This is Music in Our Schools Month. Music was made part of the curriculum in American public schools starting in 1938. If you would like more information about music as it is used in the schools, write to:

Music Educators National Conference
1902 Association Drive
Reston, Virginia 22091

✎ **Write about the music program at your school. What kinds of things are available — Choir? Band? Orchestra? Music classes? Lessons in playing instruments or singing? Which ones are you active in?**

MARCH 3

On March 3, 1931, the United States Senate passed a bill saying that "The Star-Spangled Banner" would be the U.S. National Anthem. The bill then went to President Herbert Hoover for his signature. The President signed it the same day, and it became a law. "The Star-Spangled Banner" has been the U.S. National Anthem ever since.

✎ **Some people think that "The Star-Spangled Banner" is old-fashioned or** too difficult to sing. They feel that another song should be our National Anthem. What do you think? Should we keep "The Star-Spangled Banner" or get a new National Anthem? Explain your choice.

MARCH 4

Until the 20th Amendment to the U.S. Constitution was ratified on January 23, 1933, March 4 was Presidential Inauguration Day. The 20th Amendment changed this to January 20.

On January 20, 1841, William Henry Harrison became the ninth president of the United States. He didn't wear a hat for the cold, rainy outdoor ceremony, caught a cold, and became ill. He never recovered, and 30 days later he became the first President to die while in office.

What are your rules about bad-weather wear? If you don't have any bad-weather wear rules, invent some that make sense.

MARCH 5

"Eight hours' labor, eight hours' recreation, and eight hours' rest." These words are chanted in Eight-Hour Day parades and celebrations held in Tasmania, Australia, on this day. Each of Australia's six states has its own Labor Day, which celebrates improvements in working conditions and hours. In Tasmania, by 1890 all occupations had won an eight-hour day, and Tasmanians celebrate that today.

Do you get eight hours of sleep every night? If not, what are your sleep habits and why?

MARCH 6

Michelangelo di Lodovico Buonarroti Simoni was born on this day in 1475. Michelangelo was an Italian sculptor, painter, architect, and poet. His most famous works include his marble statues of *Moses* and *David*, his paintings in the Sistine Chapel in Rome, and the cupola of Saint

Peter's basilica in the Vatican. Michelangelo died on February 18, 1564.

✏️ What is your favorite artistic "medium" — meaning, what materials do you like to work with most? Paints? Crayons? Pencils? Clay? Watercolors? A camera? Something else? Write about some of your artwork.

MARCH 7

This is Burbank Day, commemorating the birth of Luther Burbank in Lancaster, Massachusetts, in 1849. Luther Burbank was an American naturalist and plant breeder who was responsible for over 600 different plant varieties. His birthday is sometimes combined with Bird Day or Arbor Day. Luther Burbank died on April 11, 1926.

✏️ Do you like to work with soil and plants? Have you ever grown anything of your own? Sometimes elementary teachers have their students plant seeds to watch them grow. Have you ever done anything like that? Write about your experiences with plants.

MARCH 8

Today is International (Working) Women's Day. Created to honor women, especially working women, it is believed to commemorate an 1857 march and demonstration in New York City by female garment and textile workers. International (Working) Women's Day was first proclaimed at an international women's conference held in Helsinki, Finland, in 1910.

It may be the most widely observed holiday of recent origin. Many countries around the world observe it, including socialist countries. In the Soviet Union and China, it is a national holiday, and flowers or gifts are presented to women workers.

✏️ Many kids have moms who have jobs or careers. How do you feel about this, and why? Does your mom have a job or career?

MARCH 9

Yuri Alexseyevich Gagarin was a Russian cosmonaut and the first man to travel in space. On April 12, 1961, he orbited the Earth once, traveling 187 miles above its surface. (Alan Shepard Jr., the first American astronaut in space, lifted off on May 5, 1961.)

Gagarin was born on this day in 1934. He died on March 27, 1968 in a plane crash. After his death, the Yuri Gagarin museum was established in the house where he spent his childhood.

✎ **Would you like to be the "first" to do something? How do you think being the "first" would feel? What specific thing would you like to be the "first" to do?**

MARCH 10

On this day in 1876, Alexander Graham Bell made the first telephone call — to his assistant, Thomas Watson, in the next room. His message was simple: "Mr. Watson, come here, I want you."

The first cross-continental telephone conversation occurred on January 25, 1915,

when Bell once again called his assistant, Thomas Watson. Bell was in New York; Watson was in San Francisco. The first transatlantic telephone cable went into operation on September 25, 1956.

✎ **What are the telephone rules at your house? Describe them, then tell what you like or don't like about them.**

MARCH 11

The legendary blizzard of 1888 hit the Northeastern part of the United States on this date. The severe cold, strong winds, and heavy snowfall lasted for three days, ending on March 14. By the time the blizzard was over, 400 people had died.

Because of this storm, telephone wires were placed underground in New York and other major cities, and subways (underground transportation) were planned for New York and Boston that were later built.

✎ Each year, severe storms hit some part of the world. Imagine that you are walking alone in a storm. Describe what you see, what you hear, and how you feel.

MARCH 12

Charles Cunningham Boycott was born in Norfolk, England, on March 12, 1832. His last name is now part of the English language. Here's how it happened:

Boycott was an estate agent in County Mayo, Ireland. His job was to manage land for an owner who lived somewhere else. Crops were bad, and the people were having trouble paying their rents. When they asked Boycott to reduce the rents, he did not try to help them. Instead, he served them all with eviction notices! The people got back at Boycott by refusing to allow any traffic to go through their farms or to harvest crops for him. They also refused to deal with Boycott anymore. Since their farms surrounded Boycott's home and nothing could go through them, Boycott was forced to lower the rents.

✎ To boycott something today means to have nothing to do with it. For most people, it means not buying certain products, or products made by certain companies. A few years ago, people boycotted grapes and other foods because they were not picked by union workers. More recently, many people boycotted products made by the Hormel company. What are your views on boycotting? When is boycotting a good thing to do, and when is it not a good thing to do? Would you ever take part in a boycott?

MARCH 13

Percival Lowell was an American astronomer and founder of the Lowell Observatory in Flagstaff, Arizona. He was born on March 13, 1855 in Boston, Massachusetts.

For more than 100 years before Lowell's birth, astronomers had been looking for another planet beyond

Neptune. There were many reasons to believe there was another planet out there. In 1905, Lowell started searching for the mystery planet. He died in 1916, still searching. Finally, in 1930, pictures of the sky that had been taken a week apart showed that a very faint point had moved! The newly discovered planet was named Pluto.

Pluto is small and very cold. Its day is equal to about 6½ Earth days. Its year is equal to 284.4 Earth years. The discovery was announced on Lowell's birthday, March 13, 1930, by the Lowell Observatory.

✎ **Some people use mnemonics to help them remember things. Mnemonics are "formulas" for improving the memory. For example, let's say you want to remember the names of the planets in order, starting with the one closest to the sun. The planets are Mercury, Venus, Earth, Mars, Jupiter, Saturn, Uranus, Neptune, and Pluto. Your mnemonic might be, "Mom, Vernon Elias Made Jay Sleep Under Nathan's Piano." (A mnemonic doesn't have to make sense, it just has to be easy to remember.) Write your own mnemonic for the planets. Keep it simple!**

MARCH 14

Albert Einstein was born in Ulm, Germany, on this day in 1879. He later became an American citizen. Einstein was a theoretical physicist who is best known for his Theory of Relativity, $E=mc^2$. He won a Nobel Prize in 1921. It is said that he did not do very well in math while he attended school. He died in Princeton, New Jersey, on April 18, 1955.

✎ **Einstein once said, "Imagination is more important than knowledge." What do you think he meant?**

MARCH 15

The Roman emperor Julius Caesar was assassinated on this day — the Ides of March — in 44 B.C. Earlier he had named himself Dictator for Life of the Roman Empire, and many people were upset. A conspiracy was formed, made up mostly of his friends and students, and one of them is said to have stabbed him to death.

Caesar was quite an author and wrote a number of commentaries that are still considered masterpieces. He helped Cleopatra gain and keep the Egyptian throne. With the help of Sosigenes, he reformed the calendar, and the result was one of his greatest contributions to history. His Julian Calendar led to the Gregorian Calendar, the one we use today.

✎ **Of all the days in the calendar year, which is your least favorite and why?**

MARCH 16

Since 1962, the third week in March has been National Poison Prevention Week by Presidential proclamation. It was established to encourage the American people to learn the dangers of accidental poisoning. If you would like more information, write to:

Poison Prevention Week Council
Box 1543
Washington, D.C. 20013

✎ **What can you do at home to prevent a family member or pet from being accidentally poisoned?**

MARCH 17

Today is St. Patrick's Day in memory of the patron saint of Ireland, Bishop Patrick (A.D. 389-461). In about A.D. 432, Bishop Patrick left his home in the Severn Valley of England to introduce Christianity into Ireland. In Ireland, today is considered a holiday and a holy day. "Wearers of the green" in many countries celebrate this day with parades and parties. New York City has held a big celebration since 1762. The shamrock is the traditional symbol of the day.

✎ **Describe your favorite green thing. Do you like to wear it, eat it, sit on it, or spend it?**

MARCH 18

Today is the anniversary of the first space walk. Wearing a special suit, Soviet cosmonaut Colonel Aleksei A. Leonov stepped out of his space capsule, *Voshkod 1*, for 10 minutes in 1965.

The first American to walk in space was astronaut Edward H. White. His 20-minute EVA (extra-vehicular activity) took place during the *Gemini 4* flight, which was launched on June 3, 1965, and orbited the Earth 62 times.

✏️ **Imagine that you are an astronaut on a mission in space. Describe your own 30-minute space walk.**

MARCH 19

Each year on this day, in San Juan Capistrano, California, the swallows return from their stay in the south. This traditional sign of spring has been observed since 1776 as Swallows Day.

✏️ **Invent a holiday to celebrate something you've been doing for a long time. Be outrageous! Some examples: "Changing My Dirty Socks Day." Or "Watching Three Movies In A Row Day." Tell about the special things you would do on your holiday.**

MARCH 20

Mitsumasa Anno was born in Tsuwano, Japan, on this day in 1926. Tsuwano is in the western part of Japan and surrounded by mountains. When Anno was a teenager, he traveled to Europe and saw many paintings by great artists. Today his own art is published in his many children's books. His first, called *Topsy Turvies*, was published in 1970. The pictures change when you turn the book upside-down. Anno's books are an "eye treat."

✏️ **If you are familiar with Anno's books, pick one and describe your favorite thing about it. If you are not familiar with Anno's books, pick another picture book you know and describe your favorite thing about it.**

MARCH 21

Johann Sebastian Bach, a composer and instrumentalist, was born on this day in 1685 in Eisenach, Germany. He was born into a very gifted family, and he had 20 children himself, many of whom grew up to be noted musicians. One of Bach's most famous compositions is "Toccata and Fugue in D

Minor," which you may have "seen" in the Walt Disney movie *Fantasia*.

 **What do you think it was like to grow up with so much music and so many people around? How would you feel about having a famous composer for a parent...and 19 brothers and sisters?**

MARCH 22

This is National Goof-Off Day. It is intended to be a day of relaxation, with time for some good-humored fun and some good-natured silliness.

If you had the opportunity to be silly and goof off for a whole day, what would you do?

MARCH 23

"I know not what course others may take; but as for me, give me liberty or give me death!" Patrick Henry said those words on March 23, 1775, the year before the Revolutionary War. He was speaking at St. John's Church in Richmond, Virginia, about arming the Virginia militia against the British. Because of Patrick Henry's speech, this day is known as Liberty Day.

 **In May and June of 1989, Chinese students in Beijing staged demonstrations for democracy. Many young people gave their lives for a view similar to Patrick Henry's. What are your views on freedom and democracy? Do you feel strongly enough about them that you would possibly give your life? Why or why not?**

MARCH 24

Sometime around this date, the annual Iditarod race will begin in Anchorage, Alaska. This grueling dogsled race covers more than 1,000 miles from Anchorage to Nome.

Mushers spend all year training their dogs to participate in this race, which may take from 11 to 30 days to complete.

✏️ **What is your favorite way to travel? Describe it, then tell why you like to travel that way.**

MARCH 25

Gutzon Borglum was an American sculptor, born on March 25, 1871, in Bear Lake, Idaho. You have probably seen many pictures of his most important work, and you may even have visited the real thing. The Mount Rushmore National Memorial in South Dakota was his idea. He planned the faces — George Washington, Thomas Jefferson, Abraham Lincoln, and Theodore Roosevelt — and supervised most of the carving. Borglum spent the last 14 years of his life working on Mount Rushmore. He died in Chicago on March 6, 1941.

✏️ **Many people have talked about adding another face to the four already on Mount Rushmore. If it was up to you to make the decision, whose face would you add?**

MARCH 26

According to Gene Roddenberry, creator of the television series *Star Trek*, March 26, 2228 is the birthday of Captain James T. Kirk. Captain Kirk is the commander of the starship Enterprise, the huge spacecraft that "goes where no man has gone before." His birthplace is a small town in Iowa.

✏️ **The *Star Trek* series has many fans who call themselves "Trekkers" or "Trekkies." Each Trekker has his or her own favorite episode or character from the old series, the new series (called *Star Trek: The Next Generation),* or the movies. Write about your favorite *Star Trek* episode or character. If you don't know about (or don't like) *Star Trek,* write about another science fiction story or character.**

MARCH 27

The first Nobel Prize in physics went to Wilhelm Konrad Roentgen in 1901. Roentgen was born on this day in 1845 in Lennep, Prussia. He won the Nobel Prize for discovering X-rays in 1895. Roentgen discovered that X-rays would go through certain types of material, like skin, but would not go through other types of material, like bone. With X-rays, doctors could "see inside" people to find out what was wrong with them. Roentgen died in Munich, Germany, on February 10, 1923.

✎ **Have you ever wished you had "X-ray vision"? If you did, how would you use it? What would you look at and why?**

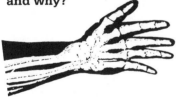

MARCH 28

In Czechoslovakia, today is Teachers' Day. It celebrates the birth of Jan Amos Komensky, a famous educational reformer. Komensky was the first person to write a book especially for children. He felt that children could remember words better if there were pictures to go with them. Czech children bring flowers and gifts to their teachers on this day.

✎ **Describe your favorite teacher. This does not have to be a teacher you have this year; it can be someone from the past, or someone you wish you had as a teacher. Why is this person your favorite?**

MARCH 29

On this day in 1886, Dr. John Pemberton introduced his invention, Coca-Cola. He described it as a "brain tonic" and "intellectual beverage."

✎ **What is your favorite kind of soft drink? How long have you liked it? And why do you prefer it over other types? If you don't drink soft drinks, write about another beverage that's your favorite.**

MARCH 30

The first pencil with an eraser attached to it was patented by Hyman L. Lipman on this day in 1858. Lipman's pencil had a groove in one end with a piece of prepared rubber glued to it.

The earliest-known pencils were used by the ancient Greeks and Romans. They wrote with flat cakes of lead on papyrus, an early form of paper. In the 1500s, someone discovered that graphite could be used for writing. The first modern pencil (like the ones we have today) was made in the late 1700s. The first pencil-making factory in the United States was built in 1861 by Eberhard Faber.

Describe your favorite thing to write with a pencil.

MARCH 31

Daylight Savings Time — DST — began today in 1918. DST conserves power and provides more usable daylight hours for afternoon and evening activities. It was adopted by the United States and other countries during World War I.

Summer DST in Europe begins on the last Sunday in March and continues until the last Sunday in September. In the United States, it begins on the first Sunday in April and ends on the last Sunday in October. The phrase "Spring forward, fall back" can help you remember what to do with your clock.

Does the change of time affect you? If yes, how? If you live in a place that doesn't have DST, do you wish it did? Why or why not?

APRIL 1

Almost five centuries ago, the New Year began on March 25 instead of January 1. At that time the New Year began on Annunciation Day, which Christians believe is the day the angels told Mary of the coming birth of Jesus. Annunciation was celebrated with an eight-day festival that ended on April 1. As more and more countries adopted new calendars and changed New Year's Day to January 1, some people decided that they didn't want to change. Those people were called "April Fools."

✎ **Play a harmless April Fool's joke on someone. Then write about your joke and how the other person reacted.**

APRIL 2

Hans Christian Andersen was born on this day in 1805. He was a Danish writer of fairy tales; maybe you know about or have read "The Little Match Girl," "The Ugly Duckling," "The Snow Queen," and "The Red Shoes," among others. In honor of Hans Christian Andersen, International Children's Book Day is celebrated on his birthday. Every two years, the International Board on Books for Young People sponsors the Hans Christian Andersen Awards to recognize outstanding authors and illustrators of children's books. If you would like more information on International Children's Book Day, write to:

The Children's Book Council
67 Irving Place
New York, New York 10003

✎ **Some book covers have descriptions of what happens inside the book. Because there isn't much space on a book cover, these descriptions are told in just a few words. Think of your favorite book or story and write a "book cover" for it.**

APRIL 3

Washington Irving was born on this date in 1783 in New York City. He was an American writer and attorney, and he served on the staff of the United States Embassy in Spain. Irving wrote "The Legend of Sleepy Hollow," a short story about a schoolteacher named Ichabod Crane, who is chased by a "headless horseman." He wrote "Rip Van Winkle," about a lazy man who wanders into the woods, takes a nap, and sleeps for 20 years. Irving also wrote many historical and biographical works. He died in Tarrytown, New York, on November 28, 1859.

✎ **Imagine what it would be like to leave home one afternoon and not come back for 20 years. What things would be different? What things would be the same?**

APRIL 4

Winston Smith is a character in a science fiction novel by George Orwell called *1984*. In the book, which Orwell wrote in 1948, a totalitarian government has taken over, ending individual privacy. One of the most famous lines from the book is, "Big Brother is watching!" In *1984*, Winston Smith breaks the law by keeping a secret diary. His first entry is dated April 4, 1984, and reads, "DOWN WITH BIG BROTHER." The book goes on to tell what happens to Winston Smith because he hates the government and breaks its laws.

✎ **Write about something you "hate." Tell why you hate it and what, if anything, you can do to change things.**

APRIL 5

Today is National Tomb-Sweeping Day in Taiwan, a holiday since 1972. According to custom, the Taiwanese people clean the tombs of their ancestors and honor them with special rites and ceremonies. During Leap Year, this celebration is held on April 4.

✎ **Write about one of your ancestors, someone who died before you were born. What have you been told about this person? How are you related to this person? Did he or she do anything unusual or become famous for any reason? If you don't know about any of your ancestors, pretend that you are descended from a famous historical figure, then write about that person.**

APRIL 6

Lowell Thomas was a reporter, editor, and radio newscaster. Between 1925 and 1976, he traveled all over the world to broadcast the news. Thomas was one of the first newscasters to report on events at the scene, while they were happening. He almost always ended his broadcasts by saying, "So long until tomorrow." He was born on this day in 1892 in Woodington, Ohio, and died on August 29, 1981.

✎ **How do you find out about the news? Do you listen to the radio, watch TV, or read the newspaper? As you are writing, include a quick overview of today's headlines so you can look back in the future and remember what happened on this date.**

APRIL 7

Today is World Health Day. On April 7, 1948, the World Health Organization (WHO) was formed. The main purpose of the WHO is to provide good health care to every person in the world by the year 2000. If you would like more information about this organization, write to:

Pan American Health Organization
WHO Regional Office for the Americas
Public Information Office
525 23rd Street NW
Washington, D.C. 20037

✎ **What are some of the biggest health problems in the world today? How are you and your family affected by these problems?**

APRIL 8

On this date in 1974, baseball's Henry Louis Aaron surpassed Babe Ruth's career record of 714 home runs. Hank Aaron finished his career with 755 home runs. He also set major-league records for runs scored, extra-base hits, total bases, and runs batted in. He was born in Mobile, Alabama, on February 5, 1934 and spent 25 years playing baseball.

✎ **Pretend that you have set a record of some type. Describe what you did. Now pretend that someone breaks your record, and describe how you feel about that.**

APRIL 9

Many Eastern countries celebrate Buddha's birthday on or near this date. In Japan, the day is called Kambutse; in Hawaii, it is called the Wesak Flower Festival and begins on the first Sunday in April. Many Buddhists call it Vesak and celebrate it on the full-moon day of the month.

Buddha was born in about 563 B.C. His name was originally Prince Siddhartha. He grew tired of the luxuries of palace life and gave up everything to travel and teach. At the age of 35, while sitting under a Bo tree in what is called "the lotus position," he meditated. It is said that he attained Enlightenment through this meditation. From then on he was known as Buddha, or "The Enlightened One." He built his teachings into the faith known as Buddhism, which is now practiced by millions of people all over the world. Buddha died at the age of 80.

✎ To "meditate" means to think deeply, to contemplate in one's mind, to ponder or reflect. Meditating is different from daydreaming. Its purpose is usually personal growth and solemn reflection on oneself. Do you ever meditate?

What kinds of things do you reflect upon? If you do not meditate, why do you think some people do? What would be some good things to think deeply about?

APRIL 10

Many annual prizes are given in the fields of journalism and literature. Among the most famous and important are the Pulitzer Prizes, founded by Joseph Pulitzer. Pulitzer was born in Mako, Hungary, on April 10, 1847 and came to the United States in 1884. During his lifetime he was a reporter, a Missouri legislator, a lawyer, a member of the U.S. House of Representatives, and a newspaper owner. He also founded the Columbia School of Journalism. Pulitzer died in 1911. If you would like more information, write to:

Pulitzer Prize Board
702 Journalism
Columbia University,
New York, New York 10027

✎ If you were in charge of giving awards to writers, what kinds of things would you look for in their writing?

APRIL 11

On this date in 1968, exactly one week after the assassination of Martin Luther King, Jr., the Civil Rights Act was signed into law by President Lyndon B. Johnson. The new law protected people who became civil rights workers. It expanded the rights of Native Americans. It also made it more difficult to discriminate against people of color in housing matters.

✎ **Many people felt that this law should have been passed many years before. Others were angry that it was passed at all. What is your opinion about the Civil Rights Act? Give your reasons for your opinion.**

APRIL 12

On this date in 1934, one of the strongest natural winds ever recorded blew across Mount Washington in New Hampshire at gusts of up to 231 miles per hour. An even stronger wind was clocked at 280 miles per hour in a tornado at Wichita Falls, Texas, on April 2, 1958.

✎ **Wind blowing that hard can be scary. Have you ever been frightened by the weather? If yes, tell about that time. If no, what kind of weather might frighten you?**

APRIL 13

"It eats thirty pounds of rice besides hay and straw — drinks all kinds of wine and spirituous liquors, and eats every sort of vegetable; it will also draw a cork from a bottle with its trunk." These words appeared in the *New York Argus* on April 23, 1796. The writer was describing the first elephant to come to the United States. It arrived in New York City from Bengal, India, on April 13, 1796. It was two years old and six and one-half feet tall. A man named Jacob Crowninshield exhibited the animal to the public.

You may have heard a folktale called "The Blind Men and the Elephant," in which six blind men meet an elephant and come up with very different opinions about it. The first blind man touches the elephant's side and thinks, "An elephant must be like a wall!" The second blind man touches a tusk and says, "An elephant must be like a spear!" The third blind man feels the trunk and thinks, "An elephant must be like a snake!" The fourth blind man feels a knee and decides that an elephant must be a tree. The fifth touches an ear and says an elephant is like a fan...and finally, the sixth blind man feels the elephant's tail and thinks, "It's like a rope."

✎ It's not unusual for different people (sighted or not) to "see" things differently. When asked to describe the same incident, they remember it very differently. Has this ever happened to you? (For example: Somehow a window got broken. Your brother "saw" you do it — but you didn't do it!) Write about an event like this from your own life.

APRIL 14

Today is Pan American Day. The beginnings of this day trace back to April 14, 1890, when the First International Conference of American States met in Washington, D.C. The people at the conference adopted a resolution which led to the creation of the Pan American Union in 1910. In 1948, the Pan American Union was renamed the Organization of American States, or OAS. But today is still called Pan American Day. It is a good day to think about peace and cooperation.

✎ Have you ever been on a trip outside the country you live in? Tell about your travels. If you have not traveled much, where would you like to go and why?

APRIL 15

Just before midnight on April 14, the "unsinkable" *Titanic* struck an iceberg. It sank at 2:27A.M. on April 15, 1912. Some 2,224 people were on board, and more than 1,500 died. The *Carpathia* reached the scene of the sinking before 3:00A.M. and rescued about 700 people from the cold water.

Because the *Titanic* sank in such deep water, no one was able to find it for many years. Then, in July of 1986, an expedition led by Dr. R. D. Ballard finally located the sunken ship. Two memorial plaques were left on the deck.

✎ Pretend that you are involved in some type of disaster. You will not be hurt, but you can only take one thing with you, something you can carry on your own. What will you take and why?

APRIL 16

Charles Spencer Chaplin was born in London, England on this day in 1889. He was a celebrated comedian who made his film debut in 1914. He was knighted by England's Queen Elizabeth in 1975 and died in Switzerland on December 25, 1977. During his career, he was known as Charlie Chaplin and also as his most famous character, the Little Tramp.

✎ **Charlie Chaplin had a very unusual, funny way of walking which he used frequently in his films. You may not walk in an unusual way, but you may have a special place you like to go to or a special path you like to use in your walking. Write about why you like to go to this place or use this path. If you are unable to walk, write about a special place you are able to get to.**

APRIL 17

This is Keep America Beautiful Month. Its purpose is to educate Americans about the problems of littering and ways to improve the environment. If you would like more information, write to:

Keep America Beautiful, Incorporated
9 W. Broad Street
Stamford, Connecticut 06902

✎ **Many families are now recycling or helping their communities by picking up trash in parks or along roadways. What does your family do to keep your country beautiful? What can you do personally?**

APRIL 18

"Twas the 18th of April in '75" is the first line of a poem written by Henry Wadsworth Longfellow about Paul Revere's "midnight ride." In fact, Paul Revere started his ride at about 10:00 P.M. He went to warn the patriots between the cities of Boston and Concord that the British were coming to invade the area.

✏️ When an author writes "historical fiction," he or she uses actual names of real people along with fictional, or made-up, characters. You may have read a work of historical fiction called *Johnny Tremain*, in which Johnny interacts with Paul Revere and other real people of the time. Write about a historical fiction book or story you have read. Tell about some of the details that made it realistic. If you can't remember reading a work of historical fiction, choose a time in history you feel would make a good story, then tell why you chose that time.

APRIL 19

On April 19, 1775, Captain John Parker gave a famous order to his troop of minutemen. "Stand your ground," he told his men. "Don't fire unless fired upon; but if they mean to have a war, let it begin here."

Captain Parker was born in Lexington, Massachusetts, on July 13, 1729. He died on September 17, 1775.

✏️ A minuteman was to supposed be ready at a minute's notice. Have you ever gotten up late and had only a few minutes to get ready before you had to go somewhere? Write about that time. What happened? Where did you have to go? How long did you have to get ready? Did you make it on time?

APRIL 20

Adolf Hitler was born on this date in 1889. He founded the German Nazi party and led his country into World War II. Hitler was obsessed with the idea that the "Aryan race" was superior to all other races. "Aryan" was a term used by the Nazis to mean a caucasian (white person) of non-Jewish descent. On April 30, 1945, when he realized that Germany was about to lose the war to the Allied forces, Hitler shot himself to death while hiding in a Berlin bunker.

✏️ "Neo" is a prefix that adds the meaning "new," "recent," or "latest" to words it is joined with. In the United States and other countries, there are people who are called "neo-Nazis." These people believe, as Hitler did, that non-Jewish whites are superior to all other races. Many neo-Nazis are young people who were not alive during Hitler's time. What are your views on neo-Nazism? Give reasons for the way you feel.

APRIL 21

Friedrich Froebel was a German educator and author who was born on this day in 1782. Froebel believed that play, toys, and music were important to a child's education. He invented kindergarten and founded the first one in 1837. He also invented learning toys.

The first kindergarten in a United States public school was founded by German immigrants in 1873 in St. Louis, Missouri.

✏ Write about your memories of kindergarten. Do you remember your teacher? What were some of the things you did?

APRIL 22

Sumardagurin Fyrsti is a national public holiday in Iceland to celebrate the first day of summer. It is often observed on the last or next-to-last Thursday in April. It began when Iceland was still using a calendar that divided the year into 26 weeks of summer and 26 weeks of winter. The old holiday traditions are no longer followed, but the day is still cause for festivities such as parades and street dancing.

✏ Describe the seasons in the area where you live. Do you have four of them? Do the seasons change at all?

APRIL 23

William Shakespeare was born at Stratford-on-Avon, England, on April 23, 1564. He died on his birthday in 1616. Shakespeare was the author of at least 154 sonnets (poems) and 36 plays, including *Romeo and Juliet*, *Hamlet*, and *The Tempest*. His birthday is a festival day in Stratford-on-Avon, and it is observed by Shakespeare enthusiasts in many nations around the world.

✏ Which would you rather do: write a play,

watch a play, or act in a play? Give reasons for your answer.

APRIL 24

Consumer Protection Week begins on or around this date each year. Its purpose is to draw attention to the ways people can be cheated when they buy things. Some of these ways are fraud and false advertising — saying a product is better than it really is, or can do something that it really can't. If you would like more information about Consumer Protection Week, write to:

The US Postal Service
Communications Department
475 L'Enfant Plaza
Washington, D.C. 20260

✎ **Write about a product you bought or received that wasn't what it was advertised to be. How did you feel about it? Or, if this has never happened to you, write about ways people can protect themselves from being cheated.**

APRIL 25

In New Zealand, Australia, and Western Samoa, this is Memorial Day, or ANZAC Day. ANZAC stands for Australia and New Zealand Army Corps. The day originally honored the soldiers who lost their lives on the Gallipoli Peninsula in World War I. In recent years the parades have honored soldiers who served in other wars, too.

✎ **There are many organizations that are called by their initials, which are easier to remember and use than their full names. Besides ANZAC, another example is NATO, which stands for the North Atlantic Treaty Organization. List as many initials and complete titles as you can. If you know, tell what each organization does.**

APRIL 26

Today marks the anniversary of the Chernobyl nuclear reactor disaster of 1986. An explosion occurred at the Soviet Union's atomic power station at Pripyat in the Ukraine. Radioactive material was sent into the atmosphere from a fire that burned for days. The accident caused worldwide concern about the dangers of nuclear reactors. More than 500 reactors are in operation around the world today.

✎ **How close do you live to a nuclear power plant? Are you concerned about the use of nuclear power? If yes, tell why. If no, tell why not.**

APRIL 27

Today is the birthday of Norman Bel Geddes. He was born in 1893 in Adrian, Michigan. Bel Geddes was an American theatrical and industrial designer. He was responsible for the early trend in functional, realistic stage designs. He was also responsible for pioneering the designs of airplane, train, and automobile interiors.

✎ **Have you ever designed anything? Have you ever drawn plans for a house, an airplane, a new toy, or something else? Tell about your design and what you liked about it.**

APRIL 28

Thor Heyerdahl, a Norwegian explorer and anthropologist, tried to find evidence that people from ancient cultures could have traveled across the oceans to start new cultures or combine with existing ones. To prove his point, he sailed the Pacific, the Atlantic, and the Persian Gulf in replicas of primitive crafts.

On this day in 1947, Heyerdahl set sail from Peru on a raft called the *Kon Tiki* to prove that the islands of the South Pacific could have been reached from the Americas. He was successful. A book about his South Pacific adventure was named *Kon Tiki*, after the raft.

✎ **Think of all the adventures you have heard about, read about, or seen films or movies of. (The discovery of the *Titanic*? A trek across Antarctica? The first moon landing?) Now pick one you wish you had gone on. Tell why you would have liked to be a part of that adventure.**

APRIL 29

Rod McKuen's birthday is today. He was born in San

Francisco in 1933. McKuen is a famous contemporary American poet who usually writes about his personal feelings.

 **Write a poem about anything you like. Make it at least five lines long. Remember that poems do not necessarily have to rhyme. You might try a Haiku or Tanka poem.**

APRIL 30

Tonight is Walpurgisnacht, the Witches' Sabbath. People in Northern Europe have observed this night for centuries. Long ago, they believed that witches rode across the sky, and that ringing church bells and clanging pots would prevent the witches from casting spells. In Austria, people put brooms and rakes upside-down into the ground to "snag" the witches as they flew by. In Sweden, bonfires were lit to keep the witches away. This festival really just welcomed spring.

Most people get ready for spring by planting flowers, fertilizing the grass, or doing some spring cleaning. What is your family's way of getting ready for spring? What do you do to help?

MAY 1

International Labor Day, or Workers' Day, is celebrated in more than 60 nations today. Canada and the United States celebrate Labor Day in September. Some nations call today May Day, others call it Eight-Hour Day, and some call it an International Day of Solidarity of the Working People.

✎ **What kind of job do you think you'd like to have when you finish school? Give reasons for your choice.**

MAY 2

Henry Martyn Robert was an American army officer and military engineer. He was born on May 2, 1837. He is remembered today as the author of *Robert's Rules of Order*, a book that outlines how people should act during meetings. General Robert wrote his book in 1876 and based it on the ways the British Parliament ran its meetings. The book spells out specific procedures for things like bringing up new ideas, voting, and speaking out during meetings. These procedures help meetings to be organized and orderly.

Over the years, the rules of keeping order during meetings have changed, and so has Robert's book. Many companies and organizations use Robert's Rules to guide their meetings.

✎ **Why is it important for meetings to be organized and orderly? What happens when they aren't?**

MAY 3

Chicago's Museum of Science and Industry used to be a Palace of Fine Arts building. It was originally part of the World's Columbian Exposition, which opened in Chicago on this day in 1893. The largest Ferris wheel ever built was part of the exposition. It was 250 feet in diameter and had 36 cars which held 60 people each. Over a thousand people could ride on it at the same time! It was invented just for the fair by George Washington Gale Ferris, an American engineer. Ferris was born on February 14, 1859, in Galesburg, Illinois. He died in Pitts-

burgh, Pennsylvania, on
November 22, 1896.

✎ **When you go to a carnival or an amusement park, which rides do you like to ride? Why? Which rides don't you like to ride? Why?**

MAY 4

May is National Sleep Month. Everyone sleeps for varying amounts of time, and in varying places. Some people sleep on mattresses, some on waterbeds, and some in sleeping bags under the stars. If you would like more information about Sleep Month, write to:

Better Sleep Council
Box 13
Washington, D.C. 20044

✎ **What are your sleep habits? Are there rules about when you have to go to bed? Where is your favorite place to sleep besides your own bed?**

MAY 5

Today is a national holiday in Japan. It is observed on the fifth day of the fifth month every year. Young people across the country are wished happiness and health, and each family flies special kites shaped like fish for all of their children. This tradition began when the holiday was called Boys' Day and families placed fish kites on poles outside their homes, one for each boy in the family.

✎ **How many children are in your family? Tell a little something about your brothers and sisters. If you don't have any brothers or sisters, write how you feel about being an only child.**

MAY 6

Rudolph Valentino was born in Castellaneta, Italy, on this day in 1895. His full name was Rodolpho Alfonzo Rafaello Pierre Filibert Guglielmi di Valentina d'Antonguolla. He came to the United States in 1913, worked as a dishwasher and a gardener, moved to Hollywood and started playing bit parts in films. By 1921 he was a matinee idol — a movie star. It is said that women would scream and cry when he came on the screen. Valentino's personal life was often disrupted by his female fans.

✎ **Who do you think is the modern Valentino? Are you a fan? If yes, why do you like that actor? If no, why don't you like him?**

MAY 7

In September of 1989, astronomers around the world had a lot to celebrate. The pictures of Neptune taken by *Voyager 2* had finally begun to arrive. *Voyager* traveled 12 years and 4.43 billion miles before reaching Neptune's orbit. The tiny starship will continue to send back information as it continues on through the Milky Way.

Today could begin Astronomy Week. Astronomy Week is observed during the week in which Astronomy Day falls. Astronomy Day is observed on the Saturday nearest to the first quarter moon between mid-April and mid-May. If you would like more information

(and this year's dates for Astronomy Day and Astronomy Week), write to:

The Astronomical League
Gary E. Tomlinson, Coordinator
c/o Chaffee Planetarium
54 Jefferson Avenue SE
Grand Rapids, Michigan 49503

✎ **Is it important to study the stars? Why or why not? What is your favorite part of the night sky?**

MAY 8

Jean Henri Dunant was the founder of the Red Cross Society. He was born in Geneva, Switzerland, on May 8, 1828. He won a Nobel Prize in 1901. In 1862, Dunant published an article describing the sufferings of the wounded during the war. He requested that an organization be established to help those people. This request led to the establishment of the Red Cross. Today the Red Cross symbol is known all over the world.

✎ **Give some examples of where the Red Cross might have gone and helped during the last two months. Tell what they could have done.**

MAY 9

Sir James Matthew Barrie was a Scottish playwright and novelist. He wrote a book of stories called *The Little White Bird*. One of the stories was about a boy who refused to grow up. In 1904, Barrie wrote a play based on his story and called it *Peter Pan*. His play included many special effects that had not been used before on the stage. For example, the person who played Peter had to "fly" across the stage. But first the actor had to make sure that his or her insurance was paid!

Barrie's *Peter Pan* has been made into a full-length cartoon by the Disney Studios. It has also been performed in many different places and on television.

✎ **Would you like never to grow up — to stay a kid forever, like Peter Pan? What age would you stay at if you had the choice?**

MAY 10

The first official Mother's Day was held in Philadelphia, Pennsylvania, in this day in 1908. For at least a year before then, Julia Ward Howe and Anne Jarvis had been going to public meetings and churches, suggesting ways to give mothers national recognition. On May 9, 1914, President Woodrow Wilson issued a proclamation making the second Sunday in May Mother's Day in the United States.

✎ **Write about your mother. If you don't have a mother, write about another woman who takes that role in your life. Tell something you admire about her.**

MAY 11

Today marks the date that Minnesota was admitted to the United States in 1858. It was the thirty-second state.

One of Minnesota's nicknames is "Land of 10,000 Lakes." Some estimates place the total number of lakes in the state as high as 22,000! Together they take up more than 4,750 square miles. Leech Lake and Lake Mille Lacs are among the largest lakes. One of the most famous is Lake Itasca, where the Mississippi River begins.

✐ **What is your favorite lake or body of water? Describe it, using as many adjectives as you can.**

MAY 12

Edward Lear was an English poet and painter. He was born on this date in 1812. This is Limerick Day because Lear made this type of poetry popular. Remember that a limerick usually has five lines and starts with the words "There once was a..." The first two lines and the last line rhyme with each other and have eight syllables each. The third and fourth lines rhyme and have five syllables each.

✐ **Try writing your own limerick. Make it as silly as you can.**

MAY 13

Stevie Wonder made his first record, called "Fingertips," when he was only 12 years old. Wonder is a blind musician who sings, plays keyboards, and composes. He was born on this date in 1950.

✐ **Some people believe that when you lose one of your senses (or are born without it), your brain compensates by increasing your abilities in another area. Do you agree or disagree? Explain your answer. If you agree, can you give an example of a case where this is true?**

MAY 14

Today is the birthday of George Lucas. He was born in Modesto, California, in 1944. Lucas directed the *Star Wars* movies, some of the most popular films of all time.

✐ **Write a paragraph about your favorite *Star Wars* movie character. Why is that character your favorite? If you have never seen a *Star Wars* movie, write about another of your favorite movie characters.**

MAY 15

This is Peace Officers Memorial Day, to honor all the law-enforcement personnel (especially police officers) who have lost their lives in the line of duty. The week surrounding this day is called Police Officers Week. If you would like more information on Peace Officers Memorial Day and Police Officers Week, write to:

National Association of Chiefs of Police
1000 Connecticut Avenue NW
Suite 9
Washington, D.C. 20036

✎ **Write about a time when you met or spoke with a police officer. If you have never met a police officer, write about what you think it would be like to be a police officer.**

MAY 16

William Henry Seward was born on this day in 1801. Seward was the Secretary of State under President Abraham Lincoln. In 1868, Seward bought Alaska from Russia for $7,200,000. Many people at the time thought the price was too high. They called the purchase "Seward's Folly."

✎ **A "folly" is a foolish action or belief. Write about something that you think is a pretty foolish action or belief.**

MAY 17

On this day in 1814, Norway declared its independence from Sweden. Today is a national holiday in Norway, complete with parades and festivities. Many Norwegian-American communities in the United States also celebrate Syttende Mai.

✎ **What is your ethnic background? Does your family celebrate any ethnic holidays? If yes, write about them. If no, write about your favorite ethnic food.**

MAY 18

On May 18, 1980, Mount St. Helens erupted. The volcano in southwestern Washington

State sent smoke, steam, and ash 11 miles high into the sky. Then winds carried and spread the volcanic debris over parts of three states.

Just a few months after the eruption, small flowers and grass began to poke through the gray-black volcanic ash. Although the area is still dev-astated, it is slowly returning to life.

✏️ **Have you ever seen a forest or grassy area that has been destroyed by fire? If yes, describe the sights, sounds, and smells. If no, write about how you imagine they would be.**

MAY 19

Today is Youth and Sports Day in Turkey. It is a public holi-day that celebrates that coun-try's independence movement, which began in 1919 and was led by Mustafa Kemal, later known as Ataturk. Turkey wanted to be independent from Greece. Ataturk became the Turkish Republic's first President on October 29, 1923.

✏️ **Some schools have in-tramural sports programs or participate with other schools in sporting events. Have you ever played on a team? If yes, write about your experience. If no, write about a sport you might like to play someday.**

MAY 20

The International Bureau of Weights and Measures was established by treaty on this date in 1875. Nations around the world agreed to standard-ize weights and measure-ments. The Bureau is located on international territory in Sevres, France.

✏️ **Write about how much you weigh. Tell how much you weighed when you were born compared to now. How does your weight compare to others in your age group? How do you feel about your weight?**

MAY 21

In the astronomical/astrologi-cal zodiac, today is the day we enter the sign of Gemini. The zodiac divides the sun's orbit into 12 parts.

Many people believe that those born under the same zodiac sign share some common characteristics. For example, they believe that Geminis have a strong sense of awareness and good communication skills: that Leos are creative and theatrical: that people born under the sign of Aries are assertive and straightforward; that Cancers are cautious, emotional, and imaginative; that Capricorns are social and ambitious; and so on. Others feel there is no basis for those beliefs.

 **Do you know your zodiac sign, and have you ever read about it? If yes, write about some of the characteristics people born under your sign are supposed to have. If no, maybe this type of thing isn't important to you. Write about why.**

MAY 22

On November 18, 1865, Mark Twain's story "The Celebrated Jumping Frog of Calaveras County" was published in the New York *Saturday Press*. The characters in the story were a man, Jim Smiley, and his frog, Daniel Webster. Smiley claimed that "Dan'l" could out-jump any other frog around.

Today a town called Angels Camp, California, sponsors annual frog-jumping contests which are held on or near May 22. The contests attract more that 3,000 entrants from all over the world. If you would like more information about the frog-jumping contests at Angels Camp, write to:

The State of California
39th District Agricultural Association
Box 96
South Highway 49
Angels Camp, California 95222

 **Some people think that frog-jumping contests are just plain silly. Write about something that you feel is just plain silly.**

MAY 23

If you visited Rye, Sussex, England, around this day, you could have the opportunity to catch hot pennies. This is Mayoring Day, the time when a new mayor is initiated into office. Rye used to mint its own coins, and sometimes they were distributed still hot from the molds that made them. To carry on the custom of the hot-penny scramble, the new mayor tosses hot pennies to young people.

✎ **During parades around the world, candy pieces or small trinkets are thrown to the watching crowds. Pretend that you are a member of one of those crowds. Something you really want has just been tossed your way. Describe the sights and sounds around you and tell about your feelings.**

MAY 24

Today marks the birthday of Lillian M. Gilbreth. She was born in 1878 and grew up to be the mother of 12 children. She was also an engineer who pioneered what is called "time-motion study." Many industries now use time-mo-tion study to find the fastest, easiest ways to complete certain tasks. The book, *Cheaper By the Dozen*, by Frank B. Gilbreth, Jr., and Ernestine Gilbreth Carey, tells about some of Lillian Gilbreth's family life. It has also been made into a movie.

✎ **With 14 people in the Gilbreth family, it was important that things be done efficiently! Pick a task, then write about the most efficient — fast and easy — way to do it.**

MAY 25

Igor Sikorsky was born on this day in 1889 in Kiev, Russia. He became an American aeronautical engineer. In 1913, he built and flew the first airplane that had four engines. In 1939, he developed the first successful helicopter. He died in Easton, Connecticut, in 1972.

✎ **Have you ever flown in a helicopter? If yes, describe what it was like. If no, write about what you think it might be like. Or write about some of the ways helicopters are used today.**

MAY 26

Marion Michael Morrison was born on this day in 1907 in Winterset, Iowa. He later changed his name to John Wayne. Wayne starred in many movies and won an Oscar for his performance in *True Grit* in 1969. He died on June 11, 1979.

✎ **Have you ever seen a movie starring John Wayne? If yes, tell what you liked or didn't like about it. If no, write about another star whose movies you have seen.**

MAY 27

Vincent Price was born on this day in 1911 in St. Louis, Missouri. He starred in many movies, most of them scary. Some of his movies are *The Fly* (1958), *The Fall of the House of Usher* (1961), *The Pit and the Pendulum* (1961), and *The Raven* (1963). Price also did the scary laugh on Michael Jackson's song, "Thriller."

✎ **What's the scariest movie you ever saw? Tell why it was scary and what your feelings were when you were watching it.**

MAY 28

Today marks the Feast Day of St. Bernard, in honor of Bernard of Montjoux. Known as the Patron Saint of mountain climbers and skiers, he ministered to people who lived in the Swiss Alps. The Great and Little St. Bernard Passes are named after him.

During the 18th century, monks who lived in the Hospice of the St. Bernard Pass bred a special dog to help with rescue and guide work. Maybe you have heard of or seen a St. Bernard — a very large, furry working dog that can weigh up to 170 pounds.

✎ **What is your favorite kind of dog? If you have a pet dog, tell about it. If you don't, tell about the dog of a friend or relative.**

MAY 29

Some of the famous things said by President John F. Kennedy include: "Ask not what your country can do for you; ask what you can do for your country," and "For those to whom much is given, much is required." Kennedy was born on this day in 1917. He was the 35th President of the United States.

✎ **Pick one of the two quotations given, or another JFK quotation you know, and tell in your own words what it means.**

MAY 30

Nobody knows where and when the first Memorial Day ceremony was held. But we do know that Memorial Day, also called Decoration Day, has been observed in many places since the Civil War. When that war ended, General Nor-

ton P. Chipman suggested to General John A. Logan, head of an organization of Union Army veterans, that arrangements be made to decorate the graves of Union soldiers throughout the country on a specific date. General Logan issued an order to his organization naming May 30, 1868 as that date. Over 100 ceremonies were held on the first national Memorial Day. Generals Ulysses S. Grant and James A. Garfield attended one such ceremony. After that date, Memorial Day became more and more popular. In 1968, President Lyndon Baines Johnson signed a law that officially made Memorial Day a legal holiday, to be observed each year on the last Monday in May. It is also a day of prayer for permanent peace.

✎ **Describe what you and your family usually do over the three-day Memorial Day weekend.**

MAY 31

On this day in 1889 in Johnstown, Pennsylvania, heavy rains fell, bursting the Conemaugh River Dam. More than 2,000 people died in the flood, which destroyed thousands of homes. Some victims were not able to be identified, and they were buried in a common

grave in Johnstown's Grad-
view Cemetery. Since the destruction was so widespread
and affected so many people,
the term "Johnstown Flood"
now is used to describe any
disastrous event.

✎ **Describe a disastrous
event that has occurred recently. Tell where and
when it happened.**

JUNE 1

June is Dairy Month. Almost everyone enjoys some kind of dairy product, from ice cream to yogurt, milk to cottage cheese. If you would like more information about dairy products or Dairy Month, write to:

American Dairy Association, Director of Food Publicity 6300 N. River Road Rosemount, Illinois 60018

✏️ **Write a salute to your favorite dairy product. It can be a poem, a song, or a paragraph telling why you like it so much, even an advertisement.**

JUNE 2

The first week in June is traditionally "Teacher Thank-You Week." The week encourages students to let that "special teacher" know how much he or she is appreciated.

✏️ **Think of a teacher you appreciate — someone who made a difference in the classroom and maybe in your life. It can be a** teacher from this year or another year. Write a thank-you note or just a "hello" note to that teacher. Copy the note in your journal, and don't forget to give or send the real note to the teacher.

JUNE 3

On this date in 1888 (it was a Sunday), a funny poem appeared in the *San Francisco Examiner*. It told the story of a self-assured baseball player who had some problems in the ninth inning. The poem was called "Casey At The Bat," and it was written by Ernest L. Thayer. For this first printing of his poem, Thayer didn't put his name on it. The poem was printed anonymously.

✏️ **Write about a time when you didn't put your name on something. Maybe it was something you didn't want people to know you had written, or maybe you just forgot to put your name on it. What happened because your name wasn't there?**

JUNE 4

The first Sunday in June is Family Day. It falls between

Mother's Day and Father's Day in the United States, and it is meant to be a time when the whole family is honored.

✐ **How would you describe the "ideal family"? Imagine that you're part of that fictional family. Tell how many brothers and sisters you have, where you live, and what your parents are like. Or, if you think your real family is terrific, write about them.**

JUNE 5

Today is World Environment Day. On this day in 1972, the first Conference on Human Development held its opening meetings in Stockholm, Sweden. Representatives from 114 countries met to talk about the future of the environment — our water, forests, air, and animals. This conference led to the development of the United Nations Environment Program. The United Nations General Assembly marks this day with activities that encourage the preservation of a quality world environment. If you would like more infor-

mation about what you can do for the environment, write to:

The Sierra Club
Public Information
730 Polk Street
San Francisco, California
94109

✐ **What worries you most about the environment — air pollution, the destruction of the rain forests, oil spills, or something else? Is there anything you can do personally to help the environment?**

JUNE 6

Aleksandr Sergeyevich Pushkin was born on this date in 1799. He is considered to be the founder of modern Russian poetry, and there are many monuments dedicated to him throughout the USSR. The Russian people honor him on the first Sunday of June every year, gathering at the monuments and reading from his works.

✐ **Name a famous poet from your country. Do you think that poets should be honored? Why or why not?**

JUNE 7

Beau Brummell's real name was George Bryan Brummell. He was born in London, England, in 1778 and was considered a "dandy" when he grew up. A dandy is a very fastidious dresser — someone who tries to look perfect and in fashion all of the time. Brummell dressed very well, but he wasn't very polite. He often insulted powerful people. He ended his life in a charitable asylum in France after losing all of his money and saying the wrong thing too many times.

Write about a time when you have said the wrong thing. Tell what happened afterwards.

JUNE 8

Architect Frank Lloyd Wright was born on this day in 1869 in Richland Center, Wisconsin. His low, horizontal designs are famous for fitting in with their natural surroundings. Many people believe that his designs were way ahead of their time.

Frank Lloyd Wright is always referred to by his full name. (Nobody ever talks or writes about him as just "Frank Wright.") What is your full name? How do you feel about it? Do you like your middle name? Were you named after anybody — a relative, somebody famous? Would you change your name if you could? Write what your chosen name would be.

JUNE 9

"Be it ever so humble, there's no place like home" are some of the lyrics for John Howard Payne's famous song, "Home, Sweet Home." Payne was an American author and composer. He was born on this date in 1791 and died on April 9, 1852.

Do you agree with the quote? Why or why not?

JUNE 10

Maurice Sendak wrote and illustrated *Where the Wild Things Are* and many more children's books. He was born on this date in 1928. It is said that Sendak really hated school. He read well anyway, and he loved comic books and movies. He began doing his own illustrations while working in a toy store and studying the illustrations in other children's books.

✎ **Is there something you would like to be able to do someday? How do you think you might prepare yourself to do this?**

JUNE 11

Today is a state holiday in Hawaii to honor King Kamehameha I. He was born in 1737 and became ruler of all the Hawaiian Islands in 1810. This is also the birthday of Lorraine M. Dahlstrom, who was born in 1947. Dahlstrom is not really as ancient as she sounds. She wrote *Writing Down the Days*, and she's very proud of it. Nothing like tooting your own horn, hey!

✎ **Toot your own horn! Give yourself some kind of "pat on the back" for something well done. Go ahead! You deserve it.**

JUNE 12

Today marks the birthday of Anne Frank. She was born on June 12, 1929, and died in a German concentration camp sometime in March of 1945. Frank was a German-Dutch Jew who spent two years in hiding with her family during World War II. The time she and her family spent in hiding are documented in her diary, which her father found after her death. It was published with the title, *The Diary of a Young Girl*.

✎ **Anne Frank's detailed descriptions of her captivity were full of sensitivity and hope. Imagine that you and your family are in hiding from an enemy. Write an entry like Anne Frank might have written. Even if you have read her book, use your own words, not hers.**

JUNE 13

On this date in 1966, the Supreme Court of the United States made a decision on a case called *Miranda* v. *Arizona*. Ernesto Miranda had been imprisoned for confessing to a crime during questioning. However, he had not been told before questioning that he had the right to get a lawyer. The Supreme Court's decision provides legal rights to anyone accused of commiting a crime. Many police officers now carry "Miranda cards" that they read aloud to suspects, informing them of their rights.

✎ **You have probably seen movies or TV shows with scenes where "Miranda" is read to suspects. Write out as much as you can from memory. (HINT: "Miranda" begins, "You have the right to remain silent...") Then tell why you think "Miranda" is important.**

but it is a good time to honor our flag. And it is a sign that July 4 is coming soon.

✎ **You probably remember "The Pledge of Allegiance" from your early school days. In your own words, write what you feel the "Pledge" really means.**

JUNE 14

On this day in 1777, John Adams, one of the signers of the Declaration of Independence, introduced a resolution to the Continental Congress in Philadelphia, Pennsylvania. It said: "Resolved, That the flag of the thirteen United States shall be thirteen stripes, alternate red and white; that the union be thirteen stars, white on a blue field, representing a new constellation." That is why today is Flag Day. Flag Day was made official by President Woodrow Wilson in 1916. It is not a legal holiday,

JUNE 15

On June 15, 1215, King John of England signed the Magna Carta. He was forced to sign it by the English barons of the time. The Magna Carta guaranteed certain civil rights to the English people. Four copies of the Magna Carta from the time of King John still survive today. They are almost 800 years old!

✎ **Why is it important to keep old things? Does your family have anything that is old? What is it? Why do they keep it?**

JUNE 16

In a cage at Walt Disney World on this day in 1987, the last dusky seaside sparrow died. There are no more of them in existence; the species is now extinct. Dusky seaside sparrows were known to live only in a small part of Florida. In the hope that future research might find a way to bring the species back, the bird's heart and lungs were frozen to preserve the cells as much as possible.

✎ **Do you think it matters when a species becomes extinct? Why or why not?**

JUNE 17

On this day in 1972, when Richard M. Nixon was President, a break-in occurred at the Democratic National Headquarters in Washington, D.C. The Democratic National Headquarters was located in the Watergate Apartment Building Complex, and the whole series of events surrounding the break-in became known as the Watergate affair. It became a national scandal in the United States when Judge John Sirica felt that there had been a cover-up of some important facts involved

in the case. During the Watergate hearings, names such as John Dean, John Mitchell, Archibald Cox, and Leon Jaworski became nationally known. Two years later, the House Judiciary Committee began the impeachment process of President Nixon. On August 9, 1974, Nixon resigned — the first United States President ever to do so.

✎ **It seems that more and more people in "high places" are getting involved in scandals. Their stories are regularly reported on TV and in the newspapers. Do you think that stories like these should be reported to the public? Give reasons for your opinion.**

JUNE 18

On June 18, 1815, the Napoleonic Wars ended with the battle of Waterloo, a town near Brussels in Belgium. Napoleon Bonaparte, who had declared himself Emperor Napoleon I in 1812, lost the battle to a British leader named Arther Wellesley Wellington who combined his armies with those of a Prussian marshall named Gebhard Leberecht von Blücher. Waterloo was a decisive, disastrous defeat for Napoleon. Since that time, any major defeat has been called a "Waterloo." (For more about Napoleon, see page 149, December 2 entry.)

✎ **Today people say things like, "Well, that final math test was my Waterloo," or, "That swim meet was my Waterloo," meaning that they felt totally defeated by it. Have you ever had a Waterloo — something you couldn't win, finish, or accomplish, something that left you feeling defeated? If no, then write about how you think this might feel.**

JUNE 19

The first Father's Day was celebrated on this date in 1910. Today it is observed in the United States and Canada. Father's Day was started by Sonora Louise Smart Dodd, whose father had raised her and her brothers after their mother's death. She felt that her father deserved to be honored after all he had done for them. In 1924, President Calvin Coolidge made Father's Day an official holiday to fall each year on the third Sunday in June.

✎ **Write about your father. If you don't have a father, write about the person who takes that role in your life. Tell something you admire about him.**

JUNE 20

June is Zoo and Aquarium Month. Its purpose is to help and encourage people to learn more about zoo animals. If you would like more information about zoo animals, write to:

North Carolina Zoological Park
Route 4, Box 83
Asheboro, North Carolina
27203

Or talk to someone who works at the zoo nearest to you.

✎ **Many new zoos are changing the practice of putting animals in cages. They are displaying them in roomier, more natural settings. How do you feel about this? How do you think the animals feel about it?**

JUNE 21

Depending on what year this is, today (or tomorrow) marks the Summer Solstice, the day summer begins in the Northern Hemisphere. In the Southern Hemisphere, this marks the beginning of winter. In parts of Sweden, Norway, Denmark, and other areas in the Arctic Circle, the sun sets for just a few minutes or not at all.

✏️ **What are your plans for the summer? Write about at least one adventure you mean to go on or have.**

JUNE 22

Malvern, Arkansas is known as the "Brick Capital of the World." To celebrate, the residents of Malvern have an annual Brickfest that usually occurs around this time of the year. If you would like more information about Malvern or Brickfest, write to:

Malvern Chamber of Commerce
PO Box 266
Malvern, Arkansas 72104

✏️ **Write about five unusual ways to use bricks. (For example: Paint them and use them as doorstops.)**

JUNE 23

Each year, around the Summer Solstice, Scandinavian countries celebrate the beginning of summer, which they call Midsommar. They have Maypole festivals and they often party all night. Or maybe it's more accurate to say they party all day, since the sun only sets for a short time!

✏️ **Describe the best party you have ever gone to. If you have never attended a really terrific party, write about your "dream party."**

JUNE 24

Kenneth Arnold of Boise, Idaho, was accused of "seeing things" on this night in 1947. He reported seeing unidentified flying objects, or "flying saucers," over Mt. Rainier in Washington State. Investigators were never able to explain the sighting.

✏️ **What are your views on UFOs? Do you think there's "something out there"? Why or why not?**

JUNE 25

George Armstrong Custer became the youngest general in the Union army during the Civil War. He commanded the 7th Calvary against the Sioux Indians near Little Bighorn River, Montana. Custer and all 200 of his men were killed on Sunday, June 25, 1876. He became a controversial hero.

✎ **Write about a time when you were the youngest to do something. Or write about something you would like to be the youngest to do. (Remember that "young" doesn't necessarily mean under 20 years old! For example, Theodore Roosevelt was 42 when he became the youngest President of the United States.)**

JUNE 26

An important charter was signed on this date in 1945. Representatives from 50 nations around the world had been meeting in San Francisco since April 25 for the United Nations Conference on International Organization. By June 26, a charter establishing the United Nations had been drawn up. The original signers included Argentina, Australia, China, Cuba, Denmark, Egypt, India, Norway, South Africa, the USSR, the United States, and 34 more countries. The charter took effect on October 24, 1945, which is celebrated every year as United Nations Day. The UN now has more than 159 member nations.

✎ **Do you speak a foreign language? If yes, write about some ways it is different from English. If no, what other language would you like to learn and why? If English is a foreign language to you — if you are a native speaker of another language — write about what it was like to learn English.**

JUNE 27

Helen Adams Keller was born on this date in 1880 in Tuscumbia, Alabama. Just before her second birthday, she became blind and deaf. In 1887, Anne Sullivan became her teacher. Sullivan was partially blind herself, and she pioneered educational techniques for the handicapped. She was

Helen Keller's companion for many years. In 1904, Helen Keller graduated from Radcliffe College with honors. She lectured frequently and wrote many books and articles to earn funds for the blind. If you would like more information about blindness, write to:

Helen Keller International
Foundation for the Blind
15 West 16th Street
New York, New York 10011

✎ **Close your eyes for a short time and listen to the sounds around you. Then write a description of what you heard when your eyes were closed. If you are blind or seeing impaired, write about any special equipment or services you use.**

JUNE 28

If you have ever wondered why so many national holidays in the United States fall on Mondays, here's the reason. On June 28, 1968, President Lyndon B. Johnson signed a law giving Americans more three-day weekends. By January 1, 1971, Washington's and Lincoln's birthdays (which used to be two separate holidays) had been combined into one holiday called President's Day. It is always celebrated on a Monday. So are Memorial Day, Labor Day, and Columbus Day. Thanks to the 1968 law, people in the United States enjoy at least four three-day weekends every year.

✎ **Which would you rather have, a three-day weekend or a day off in the middle of the week? Give your reasons.**

JUNE 29

This has been National Tennis Month. Tennis can be played outdoors or indoors by two or four players. Modern tennis was developed by Major Walter C. Wingfield, an Englishman who combined some original ideas with older forms of the game.

✎ **Even though you may not play tennis, you probably own a pair of tennis shoes. Write a salute to your tennies. It can be a poem, a song, a paragraph telling why you like them so much, even an advertisement. If you don't own a pair of tennis shoes, write about whatever you have on your feet right now.**

JUNE 30

On this date in 1857, English author Charles Dickens gave the first public reading from his works. He read from *A Christmas Carol* to an audience at St. Martin's Hall in London. Over the next several years, Dickens gave almost 500 public performances. He even toured the United States in 1867–1868, attracting crowds to his readings. (To find out more about Charles Dickens, see page 25, February 7 entry.)

✎ Imagine that you've just received an invitation to a reading. Your favorite author will be reading from your favorite book. Name the author and the book. Then tell if you would go to the reading or not. Give your reasons. (For example, maybe you would like to get an autograph.)

JULY 1

Today is American Stamp Day. The first United States postage stamp was issued on July 1, 1847.

✏️ **This is a good day to write that letter you've been thinking about writing — to grandma, to the friend who moved away, to complain about something or to compliment someone. In your journal entry for today, tell who you wrote to and why.**

JULY 2

July is National Ice Cream Month. It is said that the explorer Marco Polo told his friends back home about flavored ice foods from the Far East — that was in the year 1295! Ice cream was first manufactured in the United States in 1851. If you would like more information about ice cream, write to:

International Ice Cream Association
888 Sixteenth Street NW
Washington, D.C. 20006

✏️ **What is your favorite flavor of ice cream? What flavor would you like to try, but haven't yet? Do you like to put toppings on your ice cream? Which ones? Pretend that you've just been asked to describe ice cream to someone who has never eaten it before. Tell what it feels like, smells like, looks like, and tastes like.**

JULY 3

July is National Peach Month to celebrate this sweet, juicy fruit. The official Latin name for a peach tree is *Prunus persica*. A peach is called a "drupe fruit" because it has a single seed. Before peach trees get peaches on them, they have decorative pink blossoms. Peaches usually have fuzzy skins, but smooth-skinned variations have recently been developed. If you would like more information about peaches, write to:

The National Peach Council
3299 K Street NW
7th Floor
Washington, D.C. 20007

✏️ **What is your favorite way to eat peaches? Do you like peach yogurt, peach cobbler, or plain sliced peaches? Write about** peaches. If you don't like peaches, write about another drupe (one-seeded) fruit that is your favorite. (For example: apricots, plums, cherries, cranberries.)

JULY 4

You already know that today is Independence Day in the United States. But you may not know that today you and the Earth are 94,510,000 miles away from the sun. That is about as far away from the sun as you will probably ever be. Today the Earth is at aphelion, the point in its orbit where it is farthest from the sun. It starts on its path back toward the sun tomorrow. On January 1 it will be at perihelion, the point where it is closest to the sun.

 Are you on any kind of personal "path"? Maybe you're starting a new book, or making a new friend, or beginning a new hobby. Write about your "path." Or write about how you and your family are celebrating the Fourth of July.

JULY 5

Around this date each year, a special eight-day festival takes place in Pamplona, Spain. It is called "the running of the bulls" because bulls are turned loose on certain streets and run to the bullring. Every morning, men show their bravery by running ahead of the bulls. They dress in white with red accents and often find themselves climbing up the walls or fences for safety!

Many states in the United States are concerned about the safety of car drivers and riders. More and more states are passing special seatbelt laws. Does your state have a mandatory seatbelt law? If yes, tell your opinion of it. If no, tell why you think your state should or shouldn't have such a law.

JULY 6

On this date in 1946, Sylvester Stallone was born in New York City. He is best know for playing "Rocky" and "Rambo" in the movies.

Have you ever seen a Sylvester Stallone movie? If yes, write a critique of it.

Tell what you thought of the acting, the scenery, and the story. If no, write a critique of another movie you have seen.

JULY 7

Tanabata, the Star Festival, is celebrated in Japan today — the seventh day of the seventh month, called the "Seventh Eve." An ancient Japanese legend tells the tale of Princess Vega and a cowherd named Altair who were very much in love, but could only see each other on the Seventh Eve. It is said that this is a lucky day for lovers.

✎ Do you have something you think is lucky? Write about your lucky shirt, lucky socks, or rabbit's foot. Tell your reasons for thinking it is lucky.

JULY 8

This is National Hot Dog Month. In some places a hot dog is also called a "frankfurter" or a "wiener." Many people think the the best way to eat a hot dog is on a long, soft bun. Some people put chili or pickles or onions or cheese or catsup on their hot dogs. Some even eat them with hot peppers and tomatoes. And some eat them with everything! If you would like more information about hot dogs, write to:

The National Hot Dog and Sausage Council
3 Westbrook Corporate Court
Suite 1000
Westchester, Illinois 60154

✎ What is you favorite way to eat a hot dog? Do you prefer a particular kind of hot dog? Write a salute to hot dogs. It can be a poem, a song, a paragraph telling why you like them so much, even an advertisement. If you don't like or don't eat hot dogs, write about another favorite food.

JULY 9

Elias Howe was born this day in 1819 in Spencer, Massachusetts. In 1846, he invented the sewing machine.

✎ Sometimes when clothing isn't sewn quite right or isn't made with the strongest thread, it tears. And sometimes that makes for an embarrassing moment. Write about a time when this happened to you. If you have never had this problem, write about a time when it happened to someone else you know.

JULY 10

Today marks the birthday of Mary McLeod Bethune. She was born in Mayesville, South Carolina, in 1875, the 15th child of 17 born to former slaves. Her parents were farmers and very poor.

In 1904, she founded the Daytona Normal and Industrial Institute for Negro Girls, which later became Bethune-Cookman College. In 1935 she founded the National Council of Negro Women. Franklin D. Roosevelt called on her to be his adviser on minority affairs.

✎ Mary McLeod Bethune became very successul despite her humble background. Sometimes people who have not had as many benefits as others still become extremely successful. What is your definition of success? Explain your answer.

JULY 11

Elwyn Brooks White, better known as E. B. White, was born in Mt. Vernon, New York on this day in 1899. For many years he wrote for the *New Yorker* magazine, publishing articles and pieces of humorous poetry. In 1945 he wrote a book for children called *Stuart Little*, the story of a little mouse. In 1952 he wrote *Charlotte's Web*, which is still a favorite among children (and adults).

✎ What is your favorite children's story? Who first read it to you, or when did you first find out about it? Do you think you will still like this story when you are grown up? Why or why not?

JULY 12

Henry David Thoreau was born on July 12, 1817, in Concord, Massachusetts. Thoreau is a very important figure in American thought and literature. During his lifetime, he was both a naturalist and a social critic. In one of his most famous essays, "Civil Disobedience," he argued that the United States should not be at war with Mexico, which it was at the time. He tried to begin a taxpayers' rebellion to protest the war. Thoreau believed that people should follow their conscience when they felt that certain laws were unjust. He also believed that people should disobey laws only if they were willing to accept the consequences.

Many people have been influenced by "Civil Disobedience," including Mohandas Gandhi and Martin Luther King, Jr.

✎ **Is there anything happening in society today that makes you feel worried, angry, or upset? Be a social critic and write about it. Tell what you think should be done about it.**

JULY 13

In 1985 on this date, 162,000 people in two live audiences and an estimated 1½ billion television watchers saw many famous musicians play their music for free. There were two concerts going on at the same time, one in Philadelphia and the other in London. The concerts were held to benefit African famine relief efforts. The event was called "Live Aid," and it raised nearly $100 million in pledges to feed the hungry.

✎ **There have been many "Aid" programs since "Live Aid." Celebrities get together for a cause and perform to earn money for it. What do you think would be a good cause for an "Aid" concert or program? What would you like to see done for this cause?**

JULY 14

The French Revolution began on July 14, 1789. A mob stormed the Bastille, a fortress in Paris where people who disagreed with the government were imprisoned and punished. To the French, the Bastille symbolized government power and oppression. This day is now called Bastille Day.

✎ **Today we have French fries, French bread, French dressing, and French perfumes, among many French things. Write about your favorite French thing. Describe it and tell what you like most about it.**

JULY 15

"Twas the night before Christmas, and all through the house..." Christmas in July? No, not really, but the person who wrote those words — and the rest of the poem, "A Visit From Saint Nicholas" — was born on this day in 1779. His name was Clement Clarke Moore. He originally wrote the poem for his own children. A house guest copied the poem without Moore's knowledge and gave it to the *Troy Sentinel* in Troy, New York. The newspaper published the poem on December 23, 1823. Moore didn't know it was going to be published, and at first he didn't even get credit for writing it. Moore died on July 10, 1873.

✎ **Has there ever been a time when someone else took credit for something you did? Write about how you felt. Or, if this has never happened to you, write about a time when you got blamed for something you didn't do.**

JULY 16

The week of July 16 is Space Week, in honor of the 1969 moon landing. *Apollo 11* was launched on this day. People all over the world watched the takeoff and waited eagerly as the ship made its way toward the moon.

✎ **How do you feel about the space program? Do you think people still care about it? Why or why not? Is the United States space program worthwhile, or should the government spend all that money on something else? Give reasons for your answers.**

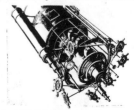

JULY 17

Douglas Groce Corrigan took off in his airplane from Floyd Bennett Field in Brooklyn, New York on July 17, 1938. He was headed for Los Angeles, but he ended up in Dublin, Ireland after more than 28 hours in the air. Upon his return to the United States, he gained the nickname "Wrong Way Corrigan." His plane had no radio or other special equipment. Corrigan did have a compass, however. He said that he just followed the wrong end of it.

✎ **Write about a time when you went the wrong way or did something the wrong way. Tell what happened and how you felt afterward. If you like, make up a nickname for yourself.**

JULY 18

July is National Anti-Boredom Month. According to *Webster's Third New International Dictionary*, something that is "boring" is "monotonous, wearisome, and tediously devoid of interest." Anti-Boredom Month was founded by Alan Caruba, who wants everyone to think about what they find boring and do something about being bored.

✎ **What kinds of things are boring to you? What do you do to keep yourself from getting bored? If someone came up to you right now and said, "I'm bored!" what suggestions would you have for him or her?**

JULY 19

Hilaire Germain Edgar Degas was a French painter and sculptor. He was born on this date in 1834. His favorite subjects for his paintings were dancers, especially ballerinas. He loved to catch them in motion. Degas died on September 26, 1917.

✎ **What kinds of dances are popular today? Pick one, then describe how you would teach someone else to do that dance. Or, if you don't dance, write about something else you do with your body that takes strength and skill.**

JULY 20

Today marks the anniversary of the first moon landing. Astronauts Neil Alden Armstrong and Edwin Eugene "Buzz" Aldrin, Jr. landed the *Eagle* on the moon's surface. and remained there for just under 22 hours. Meanwhile astronaut Michael Collins piloted the *Apollo 11* as it orbited the moon.

At 4:17P.M. Eastern Standard Time, Neil Armstrong said, "Houston, Tranquility Base here. The *Eagle* has landed." At 10:56P.M., he set foot on the moon and said, "That's one small step for man, one giant leap for mankind." Later he said that he meant to say, "That's one small step for a man, one giant leap for mankind."

✎ **Tell in your own words what Armstrong's words meant. Then tell what you might have said if you had been the first person on the moon.**

JULY 21

Ernest Hemingway was a famous American author known for his strong writing style. He wrote novels, short stories, and a novella (a short novel) called *The Old Man and the Sea*. In 1952, he won a Pulitzer Prize for *The Old Man and the Sea*, and in 1954 he won the Nobel Prize for Literature. Hemingway was born on July 21, 1899, and died in 1961.

✎ **Hemingway died because he committed suicide. He shot himself. Many people believe that handguns should be banned in the United States. What are your views on guns? Should people be allowed to have whatever guns they want? Why or why not?**

JULY 22

On this day in 1376 (or maybe it was 1284; historians aren't really sure), a story was born in Hamelin, West Germany. A famous musician came to town. He noticed that there were many rats in the town — too many. He knew that he had a special talent and could attract the rats with his pipe playing. He bargained with the leaders of the town, who agreed to pay him for getting rid of the rats. The Pied Piper did the job, but when he went to collect his fee, the leaders refused to pay him. So, the story goes, he used his special talent to lure all the children to follow him out of town, and they never came back.

 Everyone has a special talent. What's yours? Write about it and tell what you do with your talent.

JULY 23

Siddhartha Gautama, also called the Buddha, had monks who followed his teachings. He allowed his monks to own only eight things: a water strainer, a mat, a needle, an undergarment, a robe, a belt, a bowl with which to beg, and a blade. Because of the rainy season and the vulnerability of small rice plants, his monks remained in their monasteries from July to October each year. They used this time for prayer and retreat.

If you were allowed to own only eight things

for the rest of your life, what would they be? Why would you choose these particular items?

JULY 24

Amelia Earhart was born on July 24, 1898. In 1928, she became the first woman to fly across the Atlantic. In 1932, she became the first woman to fly solo across the Atlantic. In 1935, she became the first person to fly solo from Hawaii to California. Then, in 1937, she began an around-the-world flight with a co-pilot, Fred Noonan. Both mysteriously disappeared and were never found or heard from again.

Have you ever flown in an airplane? If yes, tell what it was like. If no, tell what you think it might be like to fly.

JULY 25

July is National Picnic Month. Many people enjoy packing picnic baskets, then finding some special place outdoors to eat —

a park, a lakeshore, a field in the country. Outdoor grills have also become very popular.

✏️ **If you were in charge of planning the best picnic ever, what would you make sure to have in your picnic basket?**

JULY 26

Many people have tried to develop an international language — a language that would be spoken all over the world. One of the best-known attempts is a language called Esperanto. Esperanto was invented by Dr. Ludwig L. Zamenhoff of Poland. His book on the subject was first published on this date in 1887. Today about 2 million people around the world speak Esperanto. See if you can understand this sentence: "Inteligenta persono lernas la lingvon Esperanto rapide."

✏️ **Do you think that an international language**

would be a good idea? Why or why not? What would be some of the benefits? What would be some of the problems? (P.S.: If you didn't understand the Esperanto sentence, here's a translation: "Intelligent people learn Esperanto quickly.")

JULY 27

Maybe July should be called National Month Month. We've already learned that it's National Ice Cream Month, National Peach Month, National Hot Dog Month, National Anti-Boredom Month, and National Picnic Month. Well, it's also National Recreation and Park Month. If you would like more information about parks in the United States, write to:

Park Association
3101 Park Center Drive
Suite 1200
Alexandria, Virginia
22302-1593

✏️ **Do you often go to a park or recreation area in your neighborhood? If yes, write about it. What is it like? What kinds of things do you do there? If no, write a description of your "dream park" — a park that would have everything you want in it.**

JULY 28

If you are in Gilroy, California, this year (maybe you are!), you can head on over to the annual Garlic Festival. Gilroy is known as "The Garlic Capital of the World." Visitors can sample all kinds of garlicky foods, from garlic mustard to garlic ice cream.

Garlic has traditionally been linked to superstitions. People have been known to place garlic near every door and window of their homes to keep out evil spirits. Some hang garlic outside on Halloween. It is said that if you wear a necklace of garlic buds while sleeping (that is, if the smell doesn't keep you awake), vampires won't come near you. And your soul won't be able to leave your body, so you will never be sick. It is believed that evil spirits dislike the smell of garlic.

✏ **Describe the worst smell you have ever smelled. What was it? Where were you when you smelled it? How do you think your face looked when you smelled it? What did you do?**

JULY 29

Dag Hammarskjöld was born on this date in 1905. He was a Swedish statesman who served as Secretary General of the United Nations from 1953 to 1961, a very important position. He was personally responsible for many peacekeeping efforts. He was on a peacekeeping mission when his plane crashed in what is now Zambia in 1961. Hammarskjöld was awarded the Nobel Peace Prize in 1961 posthumously (meaning "after death").

✏ **Imagine that you are a peacemaker. World leaders call on you to help solve problems between countries. Pick one problem to write about. Describe it, then give your suggestions for solving it.**

JULY 30

Arnold Schwarzenegger is an actor and bodybuilder. You may have seen him play "Conan the Barbarian" in the movies based on the comic-book character. Schwarzenegger was born on this day in 1947.

✏ **Do you do any exercises to build or strengthen your muscles? If yes, de-**

scribe them. If no, give your opinion of bodybuilding. Do you think bodybuilders look good or not? What do you think of female bodybuilders?

JULY 31

Today marks the Feast of St. Ignatius Loyola. St. Ignatius established the largest single religious order in the world. He originally wanted to be a soldier, but after being badly wounded he turned to religion. At age 33, he started going to elementary school to make up for not attending school earlier in his life. He believed that education was the best way to help people. In the later years of his life, he established many schools.

✎ Do you believe that education is important? Why or why not? What is your opinion on school dropouts? What is your opinion of people who go back to school later in life?

AUGUST 1

Herman Melville was born on this day in 1819, in New York City. He is best known for his novel, *Moby Dick*. Melville died in poverty and obscurity in 1891. His work was rediscovered in 1920 after many years of being ignored.

✎ **Moby Dick is the story of a Great White whale. Have you ever seen a whale? When? Where? Do you believe, as many people do, that whales are highly intelligent animals? How do you feel about keeping whales in captivity in zoos or theme parks? Explain your answer.**

AUGUST 2

Don't be surprised if you see a clown sometime in the next few days. This is National Clown Week. Clowns are often involved in children's hospitals or other charitable events involving children. If you would like more information about clowns, write to:

Clowns of America, Inc.
200 Powelton Avenue
Woodlynne, New Jersey
08197

✎ **Write about the last time you saw a clown. Where were you, and what was the clown doing? Do you have a favorite type of clown? If yes, tell why that type is your favorite. If no, tell why you think people like clowns so much.**

AUGUST 3

Born on this date in 1900, John Thomas Scopes grew up to be a public school teacher at Rhea County High School in Dayton, Tennessee. In 1925, he suddenly became famous. Instead of teaching his students the Biblical version of creation, he taught the theory of evolution made popular by Charles Darwin. This theory suggests that human beings developed from simpler life forms over time, and that monkeys and humans have ancestors in common.

In March of 1925, the Tennessee legislature declared that it was against the law to teach Darwin's theory — or any lessons that went against the Biblical story of creation.

In July, Scopes was put on trial, found guilty, and fined $100. (Because of Darwin's theory, this trial was called "The Scopes Monkey Trial.") He never had to pay the fine or spend any time in jail because of a technicality.

In 1967, the Tennessee law Scopes had broken was repealed. Scopes died in October, 1970.

✎ **Teachers can be very influential in their classrooms. Describe a time when a teacher strongly influenced your thinking. What did the teacher say or do? How did this affect your life?**

AUGUST 4

Born on this date in 1912, Raoul Gustaf Wallenberg was a Swedish diplomat. It is said that he personally saved 20,000 – 100,000 Hungarian Jews from the Nazi death camps by providing them with Swedish passports. He apparently died in 1947 after being arrested by Soviet troops in Budapest. In 1981, the United States Congress declared him an honorary United States citizen. Winston Churchill was the only other person to have received this honor.

✎ **Wallenberg's actions took courage. Describe a courageous act you read about, heard about, or maybe even took part in. Or define what courage means to you.**

AUGUST 5

This is National Mustard Day. Mustard comes from mustard seeds, which are taken from the mustard plant, ground up, and mixed with vinegar or oil and sometimes other spices. Many people like to put mustard on their sandwiches. If you would like more information about mustard, write to:

J. Needham
6116 Middle Lake Road
Clarkston, Michigan 48016

✎ **What's your favorite way to eat mustard? Do you put it on a hot dog, a Bratwurst, ham, or bologna, or in potato salad? If you don't like mustard, write about peanut butter, mayonnaise, ketchup, cream cheese, or something similar.**

AUGUST 6

On this day in 1945, the *Enola Gay,* a B-29 bomber, dropped the first atomic bomb that was ever used during a war. The city was Hiroshima, Japan. Over 100,000 people were killed immediately, and many more died within days. Less than 10 percent of the city was left standing. The "Peace City," an unrebuilt area of Hiroshima, has become a shrine to the dead.

What are your feelings about the use of atomic bombs? Is there ever a time when it's okay to drop an atomic bomb on a city? Explain your answer.

AUGUST 7

Magaretha Geertruida Zelle was born on this date in 1876. She was a dancer, and she was also a German secret agent operating in Paris during World War I. As "Mata Hari" (her spy name), she obtained important military secrets from high officials of several countries and gave them to the Germans. After being tried and convicted for her crimes, she was sentenced to death by firing squad. She chose to face her executioners without a blindfold, and she blew them a kiss just before they fired their guns.

Many people enjoy reading spy stories or watching spy movies or TV shows. Maybe you've seen *Inspector Gadget* or a James Bond (Agent 007) movie. There's even an episode of *Mr. Ed* where Ed the horse plays a spy — he calls himself "Oat Oat 7." Why do you think people are so interested in spies and spy stories? Do you like spy stories?

AUGUST 8

Garfield, the self-assured, lazy comic-strip cat, has a popular buddy with an unusual name. Odie first joined the "Garfield" comic strip on August 8, 1976. Odie is not very bright, and he is often fooled or tricked by Garfield.

Why do you think Garfield is such a popular kitty? What is it about him

that people laugh at? If you aren't familiar with Garfield, pick another cartoon character to write about instead.

AUGUST 9

Before the washing machine was invented, people spent hours doing their laundry by hand. They beat their clothes against rocks and washed them in streams. Or they used washboards to scrub their laundry. These methods are still being used today in many parts of the world.

On this date in 1910, the patent for the first electric-powered washing machine was granted. The first mechanical washer had been patented earlier, in 1860, by Hamilton E. Smith of Philadelphia, Pennsylvania. It had a crank that turned paddles inside the tub. The "new" electric-powered machine turned the crank using electricity. The automatic washing machine, the forerunner of the kind of washer we use today, was introduced in 1937.

✎ Have you ever had a pair of white socks that turned pink when they were accidentally washed with your red sweatshirt? Most people have experi-

enced this kind of laundry "mistake." Write about a "mistake" you know about. If you have somehow managed to escape shrunken T-shirts, suddenly-too-short jeans, or something similar, write about the laundry duties at your house. Who washes, who folds, and who puts away?

AUGUST 10

The Smithsonian Institution was established on this date in 1846. President James K. Polk signed an act making it official. James Smithson, a British citizen, had left his fortune to the United States, spelling out in his will how the money should be used.

It is impossible to see all of the Institution without making several trips to several places. Its large main complex includes the National Air and Space Museum, the National Gallery of Art, the National Museum of History and Technology, the National Museum of Natural History, the National Portrait Gallery, the Joseph H. Hirshhorn Museum and Sculpture Garden, and the National Zoological Park, to name just a few.

✏️ **When you go to a museum, what is your favorite part to "check out"? Why do you like this part? If you have never been to a museum, what kind of museum would you like to go to and why?**

AUGUST 11

"Testing, testing, one, two, three…" These are the words people normally use when they first speak into audio equipment. But on this day in 1984, instead of using these words, President Ronald Reagan said, "My fellow Americans, I am pleased to tell you I just signed legislation which outlaws Russia forever. The bombing begins in five minutes." He was only joking. He thought the audio equipment was not turned on yet. But it was, and millions of people all over the world heard what he said. Today is now called Presidential Joke Day.

✏️ **Write your favorite joke (or jokes, if your favorite is very short). Why do you think it's funny?**

AUGUST 12

"Oh, beautiful for spacious skies…" are the first five words of a national hymn almost everyone in the United States knows. The words to the song, "America the Beautiful," were written by Katharine Lee Bates. She was a writer and an educator born on this day in 1859.

✏️ **Bates used very descriptive words to talk about the United States. Use very descriptive words to write a paragraph, a poem, or a song verse about your front yard. Or write about another beautiful place you know.**

AUGUST 13

Phoebe Anne Oakley Mozee was born on August 13, 1860, in Darke County, Ohio. She grew up to be an excellent markswoman — someone who really knew how to shoot. As "Miss Annie Oakley," she was a star attraction of Buffalo

Bill's Wild West Show. She beat Frank E. Butler in a shooting match to begin her career. Butler was a national rifle champion. Later, Frank and Annie got married.

✎ **Often young women do less than their best in contests with young men. For various reasons, they feel that they should be and act inferior to men. Write about your views on this topic.**

AUGUST 14

On August 14, 1765, two effigies were hung in a Boston, Massachusetts elm tree. An effigy is a stuffed figure representing someone or something you are protesting against. (For example, in countries that don't like the United States, there are demonstrations where Uncle Sam is hung in effigy.) The elm tree in Boston became known as the Liberty Tree.

✎ **If you were in charge of making an effigy, whose effigy would you make? Who or what would you protest against?**

AUGUST 15

This day marks the actual completion of the Transconti-

nental Railway in 1869. The official celebration was held earlier, on May 10, 1869, in Promontory Point, Utah. It was called Golden Spike Day. To make the Transcontinental Railway, the Union Pacific Railroad built westward from Omaha, Nebraska, and the Central Pacific Railroad built eastward from Sacramento, California. The two railroads met near Strasberg, Colorado.

Before the time of the Transcontinental Railway, railroad tracks were not standardized. For example, some railroads built tracks 5 feet wide, and other railroads built tracks 4 feet 9 inches wide. Cars from one railroad couldn't travel on the tracks of another railroad. The Transcontinental Railway was built at 4 feet 8½ inches wide, and that became the standard. From then on, all railroads built their tracks 4 feet 8½ inches wide.

✎ **Have you ever ridden on a train? If yes, write about your experience. If no, describe a train trip you would like to take someday.**

AUGUST 16

Duncan Phyfe died on this date in 1854. He was an American furniture and cabinetmaker. His specialty was furniture made of mahogany, satinwood, maple, and rosewood. Many people today have valuable antiques that were built by Duncan Phyfe.

✏️ **What is your favorite piece of furniture? Is it a table at your house, or grandma's extra bed? Write a complete description of the piece of furniture. Tell where it is and why you like it.**

AUGUST 17

Gold was discovered in Bonanza Creek on this day in 1896. Bonanza Creek is a tributary of the Klondike River in the Yukon Territory. Even though there was a rich deposit of gold there, the harsh climate kept many people away, and the Yukon today is still relatively unpopulated. In Canada, the nearest Monday to this date is celebrated as Discovery Day.

✏️ **You are walking along a creek one day when you see a bright, gleaming object. You pick it up. It really looks like a chunk of gold! What do you do next?**

AUGUST 18

On this day in 1914, President Woodrow Wilson issued a statement to the American people. He told them that he wanted America to stay neutral in World War I, which many European countries were fighting. He did not think America should get involved in that war. Eventually, as you know, America did get involved. Over 53,000 American soldiers died in World War I.

✏️ **Write about a time when your friends were having a disagreement and you didn't want to take sides. What was the disagreement about? How long did it last? What happened? Or write about a time when you did have an argument with one or more friends.**

AUGUST 19

Today is National Aviation Day, in honor of Orville Wright's birthday in 1871. Wright was an American aviator and inventor. He and his brother, Wilbur, made the first self-powered airplane flights in history, at Kitty Hawk, North Carolina, on December 17, 1903. Orville made the first flight, which lasted for 12 seconds. During a fourth flight later that same day, Wilbur stayed in the air for 59 seconds. (For more about the Wright Brothers, see pages 155–156, December 17 entry.)

✎ **If you could fly anywhere in the world, where would you go? And why would you go there?**

AUGUST 20

On this date in 1895, the Smithsonian Institution's National Museum of American History was given the original Xerox photocopying machine. It is now part of the Smithsonian's exhibits. The photocopying machine was introduced to the public in March, 1960. It was invented by Chester Floyd Carlson, a patent lawyer.

✎ **It seems that every day brings a new invention or innovation — a new idea, device, or way of doing something. Describe an invention or innovation that you feel will be particularly important or helpful in the years to come.**

AUGUST 21

Hawaii became the 50th state on this date in 1959. Here are some interesting facts you may not know about Hawaii. It is actually a chain of 132 islands that stretch 1,523 miles across the Pacific Ocean. There are eight main islands, located mostly at the southeastern end of the chain. Hawaii has many volcanoes; the largest inactive crater, located on the island of Maui, measures 3,000 feet deep and 20 miles wide. The Hawaiian alphabet only has 12 letters: A, E, H, I, K, L, M, N, O, P, U, and W. And Mount Waialeale on the island of Kauai receives an average of 460 inches of rain per year, making it the wettest place on Earth.

✎ **Have you ever been to Hawaii? If yes, write about the highlights of your trip. If no, tell five reasons why you might want to visit Hawaii someday.**

AUGUST 22

The World Series of Little League is held around this time each year. Teams from the United States and foreign countries gather to compete. If you would like more information about the Little League, write to:

Little League Headquarters
Box 3485
Williamsport, Pennsylvania
17701

✎ **Have you ever played an "organized" sport — a sport run by a league, a park system, or some other organization? What did you play? Did you enjoy it? Why or why not? If you** could "organize" any sport into teams and tournaments, which sport would you pick and why?

AUGUST 23

Oliver Hazard Perry was born on this day in 1785. Perry is famous for defeating the British during the War of 1812. On the night of September 10, 1812, he sent a message to General Harrison saying, "We have met the enemy, and they are ours." Perry's ship, the *Lawrence*, was so badly damaged during battle that he rowed to the *Niagara*, another American vessel, and continued directing the battle from there. He died of yellow fever in Venezuela in 1819.

✎ **In his comic strip "Pogo," Walt Kelly once wrote, "We have met the enemy and he is us." Has there ever been a time when you were your own "worst enemy"? Tell what happened, what you did, and how you felt afterward.**

AUGUST 24

This is the week that many state fairs open all across the United States. Fairs usually have agricultural displays, carnival rides, animal exhibits, and entertainers. Often prizes are given for crafts, home-made foods, and works of art.

✎ **Have you ever been to a state fair? When and where? What did you like about it? What didn't you like about it? What was your favorite part of the fair? If you have never been to a fair, write about a carnival or an amusement park you have visited and enjoyed.**

AUGUST 25

Samantha Smith, an American girl, was 10 years old when she wrote a letter to Russian leader Yuri Andropov. Her letter told about her wish for world peace. Andropov answered her letter personally. He invited Samantha to visit Russia, which she did. On this date in 1985, Samantha was killed in a plane crash along with her father.

✎ **Think of a world leader you might want to write a letter to. Who would you pick and why? What would you say? If you like, write**

a real letter, ask your teacher to help you find the address, and mail it!

AUGUST 26

Geraldine Anne Ferraro was born on this date in 1935. She was the first woman in the United States to be nominated for a high political office. Democratic Presidential candidate Walter Mondale invited her to run for Vice President in the 1984 election. She became a member of Congress in 1978. Before then, Ferraro was a school teacher and an attorney.

✎ **Many school teachers go into politics. Do you know a teacher who would make a good politician? What office do you think that teacher should run for? Would you vote for her or him? Why?**

AUGUST 27

Lyndon Baines Johnson was the 36th President of the United States. He took office on November 22, 1963, after John F.

Kennedy was assassinated. He was born on this date in 1908.

Johnson began his political life as a Democratic congressman from Texas. As President, he was responsible for "pushing" Congress to enact a number of important social programs including Medicare, Voting Rights reforms, the Department of Transportation, and the Department of Housing and Urban Development (HUD). Some of these programs were begun by President Kennedy before his death.

Johnson was sharply criticized for supporting the Tonkin Gulf Resolution, which gave him and future Presidents the authority "to take all necessary measures to repel any armed attack against the forces of the United States." That resolution led to increased American involvement in the Viet Nam War.

Many people believed that the Tonkin Gulf Resolution gave Presidents far too much power. It was repealed by Congress on January 13, 1971.

✎ **Sometimes when you do something that other people disagree with or don't approve of, they forget about all of the good things you've done before. Can you think of a time when this happened to you? Maybe your parents caught you the one time you pushed your sister into a puddle instead of helping her around it. Or maybe your big brother found out about the one time you borrowed something of his without asking. Tell about this time and how you felt.**

AUGUST 28

Dr. Martin Luther King, Jr. gave a very famous speech on this date in 1963. In honor of his "I Have a Dream" speech, given during the March on Washington, this is Dream Day. Dr. King's dream was that all races could live, work, and play as equals, and that his children would grow up in such a world. His speech gave new energy to the American civil rights movement. If you would like more information about Dream Day and Dr. Martin Luther King, Jr., write to:

Global Committee Commemorating King Days of Respect
PO Box 21050
Chicago, Illinois 60621

✎ **What is your dream? Is it for world peace, no more hunger, no more poverty? Or is your dream more personal — a dream for happiness, riches, or fame? Write about your dream.**

AUGUST 29

This is According to Hoyle Day, in honor of Edmond Hoyle. His birthday is unknown, but we do know that he died on this date in 1769. Hoyle became England's leading authority on the rules of card games and chess. He wrote several articles about instructions for various games. He also compiled a book of rules and instructions for many different kinds of games, and a revised version is still being printed and used. Today, when people talk about doing something "according

to Hoyle," they mean doing it the fair, correct way.

✎ **When was the last time you were playing a game with someone and had to stop to check the rules? What were you playing, and who were you playing with? What rule did you have to check? Or write about a new game you recently learned to play. Tell some of the rules.**

AUGUST 30

"Share Our Wealth: Every Man A King" was the slogan of a flamboyant politician named Huey Pierce Long. Long was born on this day in 1893. He was elected governor of Louisiana in 1928 and became a U.S. Senator in 1930. He called for many reforms to benefit the poor. In 1935, he became a candidate for President.

During his Presidential campaign, Long promoted a program to give every family a guaranteed income of $5,000 (a lot of money in those days). He said that if someone earned more than $1 million a year, the government should take the rest. And he said that if someone inherited more than $5 million, the government should take the extra.

Long was assassinated on September 8, 1935, in Baton Rouge, Louisiana. He was shot to death by Dr. Carl Austen Weiss, who was then killed by Long's bodyguards.

✎ Huey Long was not very popular among rich people. If you were a rich person at the time Long was running for President, how do you think you would have felt about his proposals? How would you have felt if you were poor? Do you think that rich people should be forced to give money to help poor people?

AUGUST 31

California is famous for its earthquakes. But how often have you heard of an earthquake happening in South Carolina? On August 31, 1886 in Charleston, South Carolina, an earthquake did happen. It was the first major quake ever to be recorded in the eastern United States.

✎ You may not have earthquakes where you live. Different natural disasters seem to happen in different parts of the country. Maybe your part has tornadoes, hurricanes, forest fires, droughts, floods — even volcanic eruptions! Write about the natural disaster that occurs most frequently where you live. Or write about a natural disaster you read or heard about recently.

SEPTEMBER 1

The first woman telephone operator began her job today, in 1878. She worked as an operator for 33 years. Her name was Emma M. Nutt.

✏️ **What was the best telephone conversation you ever had? What made it so special to you? Or, if you can't remember a best telephone conversation, write about someone you would like to talk to on the telephone and why. It can be anyone, not just someone you know.**

SEPTEMBER 2

There are 211,600 beekeepers in the United States. Their 192.3 million bees produce over 227 million pounds of honey each year. If you would like more information about bees and beekeeping, write to:

The National Honey Board
9595 Nelson Road, Box C
Longmont, Colorado 80501

✏️ **Do you like honey? What is your favorite way to eat it — on bread, on cereal, mixed with yogurt and fruit? Write about how you like to eat honey. Or, if you don't eat honey, write about** your favorite sweet food and tell when you eat it.

SEPTEMBER 3

On or near this day, most Americans can tune into a TV program that has been broadcast over Labor Day weekends for many years. It is the *Jerry Lewis Labor Day Telethon for Muscular Dystrophy*.

Muscular Dystrophy is a hereditary disease in which the skeletal muscles waste away over time. The skeletal muscles hold the bones of the skeleton together. The disease seriously affects body movement and posture. If you would like more information about Muscular Dystrophy and the Telethon, write to:

Muscular Dystrophy
Association
810 Seventh Avenue
New York, New York 10019

✏️ **What is your opinion of this kind of fundraising? Do you think that a telethon is a good way to raise money for a good cause? Why or why not?**

SEPTEMBER 4

On this day in 1933, 10-year-old Barney Flaherty answered an advertisement for newspaper carriers. He was hired as the first carrier for *The New York Sun*. That is why today is Newspaper Carrier Day.

✎ **Have you ever had a job — newspaper carrier, babysitter, lawn mower, snow shoveler? Tell about your experiences. Do you think it's a good idea for kids to have money-making jobs? Why or why not?**

SEPTEMBER 5

The first time Labor Day was observed in the United States was on Tuesday, September 5, 1882, in New York City. On June 28, 1894, President Grover Cleveland made the first Monday in September the official Labor Day, a national holiday. Labor Day is also observed in Canada.

✎ **For many students, Labor Day is the last "free" day before school starts. How do you feel about school beginning this year? What are you looking forward to? What are you not looking forward to?**

SEPTEMBER 6

September is National Clock Month. Clocks are an important part of everyone's day. If you would like more information about clocks, write to:

Clock Manufacturers and
Marketing Association
710 E. Ogden Avenue
Suite 113
Naperville, Illinois 60540

✎ **Which do you like better, digital clocks or analog clocks (clocks with hands)? Do you own a watch? Is it digital or analog? What's the craziest or most colorful clock or watch you have ever seen? Is there a particular kind or brand of watch you would like to have someday?**

SEPTEMBER 7

Anna Mary Robertson Moses was born on this date in 1870. She became a famous painter, even though she did not begin painting until she was 78. On her 100th birthday, September 7 was officially named Grandma Moses Day. Grandma Moses died when she was a little over 101 years old. Most of her paintings were farm scenes.

✏️ **Is there anything you wish you had learned to do when you were younger? Or is there anything you wish you had done when you were younger? What kept you from learning or doing this thing? Do you have any plans to learn or do it now, or when you're older?**

SEPTEMBER 8

This is National Cable Television Month. It's estimated that over 51 percent of American homes are wired for cable television. More than 40 million people subscribe to cable TV. Some American families can watch more than 80 TV channels.

Most cable companies reserve one or more channels for community programming. You may want to find out more about community cable — maybe you can get involved!

✏️ **Do you watch much cable television? What is your favorite cable TV program or station? If you could start your own cable TV program, what would it be like?**

SEPTEMBER 9

On this day in 1850, California became the 31st state. Here are some interesting facts about California. The hottest temperature ever recorded in the United States, 134°F, was recorded in Death Valley, California. The lowest point in the United States, 282 feet below sea level, is also in Death Valley, near Badwater. The tallest tree in the United States is in California's Redwood National Park. The world's largest living thing — the General Sherman tree, 275 feet tall and 103 feet in diameter — is located in Sequoia National Park. (It may also be the world's oldest living thing. The General Sherman is estimated to be 2,500 years old!) And the San Francisco Streetcar System was the first of its kind in the United States. It was installed in 1873.

Tourism is a big industry in California. If you would like more information, write to:

California Office of Tourism
PO Box 9278
Van Nuys, California 91409

✏️ **If you were a tourist in California, what would you want to see? Where would you want to go? What would you want to do? If you have already** been to California, write about your experiences. If you live in California, write about the places that make your state special.

SEPTEMBER 10

This is Swap Ideas Day. Be creative! That's what Robert L. Birch, the person who invented this day, wants people to do on it. And don't just think of ways to be creative for yourself. Think of ways to be creative for the purpose of helping others. If you would like more information about Swap Ideas Day, write to:

Robert L. Birch
International Society for
Philosophical Enquiry
Box 2364
Falls Church, Virginia 22042

✎ **Write about a good idea. It can be one of your own ideas, or an idea of someone else's that you** have heard or read about. Tell what you think is so good about it.

SEPTEMBER 11

William Sydney Porter was born on September 11, 1862 in Greensboro, North Carolina. When Porter was in his 30s, he was convicted of embezzlement (a kind of stealing) and sent to prison for three years. He published several short stories while he was in prison. Instead of using his real name, he signed many of his stories with a pseudonym, "O. Henry." Porter was known to use a number of different pseudonyms. As O. Henry, he wrote stories with creative plots and surprise endings. Perhaps the most famous is called "The Gift of the Magi."

✎ **It is not easy to come up with good endings. Many writers know this! Have you ever read a story or seen a movie that you felt had a silly, sloppy, or dumb ending? Do you think you could come up with a better ending? Try, and write your ending.**

SEPTEMBER 12

Jesse Owens was born on this day in 1913 in Oakville, Alabama. A great athlete, he set 11 world records in track and field and won 4 gold medals in the 1936 Olympics in Berlin, Germany. Adolf Hitler was not very happy about Owens's victories. Owens was black, and Hitler believed that white people were superior to black people. Owens proved that Hitler was wrong, and he did it in Hitler's own country! Owens died in 1980.

✎ **Write about a person whose accomplishments you admire. This can be an athlete, a teacher, a parent, a friend, a political figure — anyone you choose. Tell what the person has done and why you admire him or her.**

SEPTEMBER 13

September is National Breakfast Month. Its purpose is to encourage you to eat a hot breakfast every day. If you would like more information about good breakfast nutrition, write to:

Great Starts Breakfasts
Communications Center
Campbell Place
Camden, New Jersey 08103

✎ **Write about breakfast at your house. What do you eat? What do other people in your family eat? Do you have breakfast together? Is breakfast on the weekends different from breakfast on the weekdays? If yes, tell how it is different.**

SEPTEMBER 14

Although George Frideric Handel was born in Germany, he became known as an English composer because he lived most of his life in England. Handel was considered a master of the Baroque style of music. He wrote an oratorio called "The Messiah" which was performed for the first time in Dublin in 1742. It is said that Handel worked for 23 straight days to complete his oratorio. He finished it on this date in 1741.

✎ **Write about something that took you a long time to complete. Was it a school project, something at** home, or something you did to help another person? Did it have to do with one of your hobbies, talents, or special interests? Write about why you did it and how long it took you to do. Tell how it turned out.

SEPTEMBER 15

Today is a national holiday in Japan. It is known as Old People's Day or Respect for the Aged Day.

✏️ **Write about an old person you know. This should be someone you look up to and respect. It can be a friend, a relative, a neighbor, or someone else you know. Tell about this person and why he or she deserves to be honored.**

SEPTEMBER 16

Today marks the anniversary of the day the *Mayflower* left Plymouth, England, in 1620. The ship had 102 passengers and a small crew. There were bad storms and rough water along the way, and some people on board wondered if they had made the right decision. They were often afraid and weren't sure they would complete the long and dangerous trip. But the *Mayflower* finally reached Provincetown, Massachusetts, on November 21, almost two months later. The Pilgrims were dropped off at Plymouth, Massachusetts, on December 26.

✏️ **Write a paragraph about something you didn't think you could do, but did anyway. Tell how you felt afterwards.**

SEPTEMBER 17

September is National Courtesy Month. Its purpose is to remind everyone that life could be more enjoyable if people were more polite to one another.

✏️ **Write about a time when being courteous paid off for you. Or write about a time when you saw someone using very poor manners. Tell how you felt during the time you chose to write about.**

SEPTEMBER 18

Samuel Johnson was born on this date in 1709. Many people consider him to be one of the greatest English writers of all time. Johnson won a place in history with his book, *The Dictionary of the English Language*. Published in 1755, it was the first comprehensive dictionary of English.

✎ **What is the most interesting information you can find in a dictionary? Don't just pick the obvious answer — definitions of words. Dictionaries often contain many other kinds of information, too.**

SEPTEMBER 19

The third Tuesday in September, which sometimes falls on September 19, is International Day of Peace. Regular sessions of the United Nations General Assembly begin each year on International Day of Peace. It is a good day to think about and work for worldwide peace.

✎ **If you could single-handedly bring peace to the world, what would you do? When you visualize world peace, what do you see?**

Many people feel that "peace is possible now." Do you agree or disagree? What would have to be done before we could achieve world peace?

SEPTEMBER 20

Upton Sinclair was born on this date in 1878. He was an American author famous for writing about social issues — conditions in society he believed needed changing. His book, *The Jungle*, which told about the meat-packing conditions in the Chicago Stockyards, resulted in the Pure Food and Drug Act of 1906. That act guaranteed the quality of food items sold to the public. In 1942 Sinclair won the Pulitzer Prize for *Dragon's Teeth*, his book about communism and fascism.

When Sinclair was a boy, he asked his mother, "Why should some people be rich and others poor?" After living 90 years, he said that he still had not found out the answer. He died in 1968. His personal papers, books, manuscripts, and other materials are now kept at the Lilly Library at Indiana University. They are said to weigh a total of eight tons!

✏️ **Many authors write about social issues. Think about some of the social issues of today, then pick one to write about. (For example, you might want to write about poverty, segregation, the homeless, drugs, gangs, or another issue that concerns you.) Can you think of any social reforms that might help to solve this problem?**

SEPTEMBER 21

Today is World Gratitude Day. The purpose of this day is to encourage people throughout the world to think positively about life, remember the things they're grateful (thankful) for, and express their gratitude. If you would like more information about World Gratitude Day, write to:

World Gratitude Day
Foundation
777 United Nations Plaza,
Suite 4
New York, New York 10017

✏️ **Write about something or someone you feel grateful for. It can be something big (your par-**ents' love, your own good health) or something small (your favorite stuffed animal or toy, a comfortable pair of shoes). You decide!**

SEPTEMBER 22

On September 22, 1903, an Italian immigrant named Italo Marchiony applied for a U.S. patent. He had invented a new mold to make a special kind of pastry that would hold a tasty dessert. Today we call this pastry a "cone," and we usually put ice cream in it.

Americans consume more ice cream than any other people in the world. Each year, more than 900 million gallons of ice cream are produced in the U.S.! One-third of this (300 million gallons) is vanilla.

There are also many ice cream confections available — frozen juice bars, chocolate-covered ice cream on a stick, frozen candy bars with ice cream inside, drumsticks, and more! In some neighborhoods, special trucks or carts go up and down the streets, bringing ice cream confections to people's homes.

✏️ **Write about your favorite ice cream confection. Tell what it looks like, where you buy it, when it's best to eat it, and what makes it fun.**

SEPTEMBER 23

You probably used a reading book in elementary school. There were a lot of reading books available for your school to choose from. But in the middle to late 1800s, everyone in the United States learned to read from the same textbooks. They were called *McGuffey's Eclectic Readers*, and they were all produced by the same man, William Holmes McGuffey. McGuffey was born on this date in 1800. You may want to ask your grandparents or other older relatives if they remember their *McGuffey's*.

✏️ **When did you learn to read? How old were you? Were you in school, or did you learn to read before you started school? Did you enjoy learning to read? Tell about the first book you can remember reading.**

SEPTEMBER 24

Jim Henson was born on this date in 1936. He is famous in many countries around the world as the creator of the Muppets.

✏️ **Write about your favorite Muppet character. Is it Miss Piggy, Gonzo, or Kermit the Frog? The Cookie Monster or the Count? Why is that character your favorite? If Jim Henson invited you to create another Muppet, what would it be? Give your Muppet a name.**

SEPTEMBER 25

The first American newspaper was published on this date in 1690. Called *Publick Occurrences Both Foreign and Domestick*, it was published in Boston, Massachusetts, by Benjamin Harris. The local authorities did not like what the newspaper said, so publication was stopped after only one issue.

✑ **Do you think that authorities should be able to shut down a newspaper? Why or why not? Write your feelings about the freedom of the press.**

SEPTEMBER 26

John Chapman was born on this date in 1744 in Massachusetts. He spent much of his life roaming the American Midwest, planting apple trees and giving seeds to others so they could plant trees, too. He was known as (you guessed it!) Johnny Appleseed.

✑ **Write a tribute to your favorite apple dish — apple pie, apple strudel, apple muffins, apple bread, apple anything-you-like. How is it prepared? Who prepares it best? When is your favorite time to eat it? If you don't like apples, write about what you eat while everyone else is eating apples.**

SEPTEMBER 27

Political cartoonists use current events and political figures as subjects for their cartoons. They use exaggeration, humor, and irony to communicate their point of view. One of the most famous political cartoonists was a man named Thomas Nast. He was born on this day in 1840. Nast created two of the United States' most popular political symbols: the donkey, to stand for the Democratic Party, and the elephant, to stand for the Republican Party. Those symbols are still used today.

✑ **Draw a political cartoon of your own. Try to make it about something that is currently in the news. If you can't or don't want to draw a cartoon, find one in a newspaper or a news magazine. Then explain in your own words what you think it means.**

SEPTEMBER 28

Confucius was born on this day in 551 B.C. "Confucius" is a translation of his given name, Kung-futzu. He was born in the Shantung Province in Taiwan and was a teacher for more than 40 years before his death at age 72. People all over the world still respect and follow his sayings and teachings. In Taiwan, today is Teachers' Day in honor of Confucius.

✎ **Describe the "ideal" teacher. What would he or she be like? What would his or her classroom be like? Be serious about this; don't just write about someone who "doesn't give homework" or "lets kids do what they want."**

SEPTEMBER 29

Today is Michaelmas Day. This day is also called the Feast of Saint Michael and All Angels. It is celebrated by Anglican, Episcopal, and Lutheran churches. The Roman Catholic church celebrates the Feast of Saints Michael, Gabriel, and Raphael. All three are believed to be archangels — celestial beings that rank above angels. Saint Michael is considered to be the head of the archangels and the general of the army of heaven. He is referred to as the "great and glorious" angel.

✎ **Write about angels. What do you believe about them? What do you think angels look like? What do you think they are?**

SEPTEMBER 30

This is Ask a Stupid Question Day. And that's exactly what you should do. Meanwhile, if you would like more information about Ask a Stupid Question Day, write to:

David Larzelere
c/o Flint Journal
200 E. First Street
Flint, Michigan 48502.

✎ **You've probably heard the saying, "Ask a stupid question, get a stupid answer." Today, try asking a stupid question and coming up with your own stupid answer. Is there something you've been wondering about? Something you don't understand? Here's your chance to solve the mystery, once and for all! Be silly, be creative.**

OCTOBER 1

This is National Pizza Month. To start it off right, here are some fascinating facts on this popular food.

The history of pizza dates back to 1000 B.C. The first pizza with cheese was created in Italy in 1889 by a man named Raffaele Esposito. Queen Margherita of Italy loved pizza, and Esposito made one especially for her with (red) tomatoes, (white) mozzarella cheese, and (green) basil — the colors of the Italian flag.

The first pizzeria in the United States opened in 1905 in New York City. It was owned by Gennaro Lombardi. From the 1920s to the 1950s, pizza was usually found only in Italian-American neighborhoods and made with fresh ingredients.

By the 1960s, pizza was being mass-produced. Today it is as American as apple pie! Frozen pizza is now one of the best-selling convenience foods in the United States. With today's emphasis on healthy foods, you can order pizza made with a whole-wheat crust and topped with broccoli, carrots, and even tofu.

If you would like to know more about pizza (and find some recipes to try at home), go to your local library and check out *The Pizza Book: Everything There Is To Know About the World's Greatest Pie* by Evelyne Slomon.

✎ **When you can have pizza any way you want it, what do you put on it? How much do you usually eat? What do you eat with it?**

OCTOBER 2

The "Peanuts" comic strip first appeared on this date in 1950. Created by Charles M. Schulz, it now appears in 2,000 newspapers. It is translated into 26 languages in 68 countries, where people of all ages enjoy it. Charlie Brown and his friends have even had their own animated TV specials. If you would like more information about "Peanuts," write to:

United Features Syndicate
Public Relations Manager
200 Park Avenue
New York, New York 10166

✎ **One of Charlie Brown's favorite sayings is, "Good grief!" Write two or** three of your favorite sayings and tell when you usually say them.

OCTOBER 3

Yesterday was Gandhi Jayanti, a public holiday in India to honor the birthday of Mahatma Gandhi. Mohandas Karamchand Gandhi was born in 1869. He became a spiritual leader and then a political leader. He was given the name Mahatma, which means "great souled." Gandhi promoted the use of passive resistance as a protest method. He was assassinated on January 30, 1948.

✏️ Describe the last time you resisted something. What did you resist, and how did you resist it? What happened next?

OCTOBER 4

Do you like *The Hardy Boys* books? How about *Nancy Drew* books? Did your parents like those books? They have been around for a long time.

Both were created by a man who was born on this date in 1862. His name was Edward L. Stratemeyer. He and a group of people called the Stratemeyer Syndicate wrote more than 800 books under 60 or more pseudonyms. Stratemeyer died in 1930, but at least four million copies of Stratemeyer Syndicate books are still in print. The characters and situations have changed in some ways to keep up with the times, but they are very similar to the books your parents (and even your grandparents) loved when they were children.

✏️ What is your favorite Stratemeyer Syndicate book? Is it a *Hardy Boys* or a *Nancy Drew?* If you don't know or don't care for these books, write about another book you enjoyed reading.

OCTOBER 5

October is National Seafood Month. The idea behind National Seafood Month is to encourage people to eat more seafood. If you would like more information, write to:

National Fisheries Institute
2000 M Street NW
Suite 580
Washington, D.C. 20036

✎ What is your favorite seafood? Do you like fish, shrimp, or lobster? What about squid or eels? Write about the one you would order if you went to a fancy seafood restaurant. If you don't like seafood, write about what you would order instead.

OCTOBER 6

George Westinghouse was born on this day in 1846 in Central Bridge, New York. Westinghouse invented the air brake, which uses compressed air to power the brakes on trains. He also invented automatic signal devices. During his lifetime, he obtained more than 400 patents for his inventions.

In June of 1871, Westinghouse started the "Saturday half-holiday" custom in his Pittsburgh, Pennsylvania factory. Before then, Saturday was a full work day for most people.

✎ What do you do on Saturdays? Do you spend the morning as a "couch potato," watching TV cartoons? Do you help with chores or yardwork? Do you participate in sports? Write about your typical Saturday.

OCTOBER 7

Today marks the birthday of Thomas James Wise. He was born in Gravesend, England, in 1859. Wise was a bibliophile — a person who loves and collects books. After he died on May 13, 1937, the British Museum acquired his library, which was full of rare editions and very valuable.

Three years before his death, Wise found himself involved in a great scandal. For years he had been selling books and pamphlets for high prices, claiming that they were worth it because they were old or rare or precious for some other reason. In fact, many of the pieces he sold were fakes! He forged them himself to raise money to buy more books for his own library. His greed led him to commit crimes and cheat people.

✎ Greed is an overwhelming desire for wealth, power, or possessions. Do you know someone you would consider greedy? Have you ever been greedy about something yourself? Explain your answer.

OCTOBER 8

This is Fire Prevention Week. On this date in 1871, the Chicago Fire began. Legend tells that it started when Mrs. O'Leary's cow kicked over a lantern in a barn. The fire destroyed much of Chicago, leaving 250 people dead and over $200 million in damages. On that very same day and year, a tragic forest fire began in Peshtigo, Wisconsin, that destroyed most of that city.

This week reminds us of the need for fire prevention all year long. If you would like more information about Fire Prevention Week or how to prevent fires, write to:

National Fire Protection Association
Batterymarch Park
Quincy, Maryland 02269

✎ Many homes today are equipped with smoke alarms, fire extinguishers, and fire escape ropes. Children learn in school what to do if their clothing catches fire (STOP, DROP, and ROLL!). What other fire-prevention techniques do you know about? What has your family done to make your home safer from fires? Does your family have a fire emergency plan? If yes, tell about it. Also, at the end of today's journal entry, write the fire emergency telephone number you should dial if there's ever a fire at your home. Ask your teacher or parents for help if you don't know this number.

OCTOBER 9

Benjamin Banneker, known as "the first black man of science," died on this day in 1797. Banneker was a scientist and a writer, a mathematician and a clockmaker, an astronomer and a surveyor (he was one of the surveyors of the District of Columbia). From 1792 to 1797 he published an almanac containing information about the positions of the planets — information he had calculated himself. Famous astronomers and mathematicians of the time relied on his almanacs.

You may think that Banneker went to college to learn so much. In fact, he was almost entirely self-taught. He did attend a local school as a child, but mostly he read books on a wide variety of subjects.

✎ **Write about something you taught yourself to do. Tell why you wanted to learn it in the first place. If you haven't ever taught yourself to do anything, what would you like to learn? Could you teach yourself to do it? How?**

OCTOBER 10

Today is Double Tenth Day in China — the tenth day of the tenth month. It is the anniversary of the day in 1911 when Chinese revolutionaries overthrew the Manchu dynasty.

A dynasty is a powerful group or family that rules a country for a long time. The Manchu dynasty had begun in 1644, when the Manchus — members of the Mongolian people of Manchuria — conquered China. They ruled it for almost three centuries.

✎ **Describe how your life has changed since you were 10 years old. Have your responsibilities changed? Are things easier or harder for you now than they were then? If you are still 10 years old (or**

younger), write about how your life has changed since you were 10 days old.

OCTOBER 11

Anna Eleanor Roosevelt was the wife of President Franklin Delano Roosevelt. She was born on this date in 1884. Because of her many humanitarian pursuits, Eleanor was called the "First Lady of the world." She was a delegate to the United Nations and a writer. In her book, *This Is My Story*, she wrote, "No one can make you feel inferior without your consent."

✎ **What do you think Eleanor Roosevelt meant when she wrote this? Rewrite her statement, using your own words. Or write an explanation of what she wrote, using an example or two.**

OCTOBER 12

At 2:00 in the morning on this day in 1492, Roderigo de Triana sighted land. He was a sailor on board the *Pinta*, one of three ships under the command of Christopher Columbus. (The other two, you probably remember, were the *Niña* and the *Santa Maria*.) Columbus was Italian, but he claimed the new land (now called the Bahamas) for Spain's rulers. The Spanish King Ferdinand V and Queen Isabella I had provided the funds he needed for his journey.

Since 1971, Columbus Day has been celebrated on the Monday nearest the 12th. (To find out why so many holidays are celebrated on Mondays, see page 80, June 28 entry.)

✏ **Like many sailors of his day, Columbus was afraid of sea monsters. He thought they might eat his boats and crews. Unlike other sailors of his day, he wasn't really worried about falling off the edge of the Earth. Write about something you used to be afraid of but aren't afraid of anymore.**

OCTOBER 13

Triskaidekophobia is a long word with a simple meaning: the fear of the number 13. It's even worse when the 13th falls on a Friday — yikes! Actually, for some people the day is a very lucky one. There is at least one Friday the 13th in every year, and some years have as many as three.

✏ **Many people have one or more superstitions. Some won't walk under ladders. Some have special shirts they wear to play golf or go to business meetings. Some are afraid of black cats crossing their path. Do you have any superstitions? Write about them. What kinds of things do you do (or don't you do) because of your superstitions? If you don't have any superstitions, then write a list of at least five you have heard about.**

OCTOBER 14

National School Lunch Week usually takes place around this time in October. It starts on the second Sunday of the month. National School Lunch Week was officially proclaimed by President John F. Kennedy in 1962.

✏️ **Everyone complains about school lunches. Instead, think back to the best school lunch you ever had. Tell what it included, how it tasted, and what made it special to you.**

OCTOBER 15

Today is National Grouch Day. A grouch is someone who grumbles and complains a lot. Other words for grouch are crank, grump, sorehead, and sourpuss.

One of the biggest grouches in history was a man named William Claude Dukenfield. He was born in Philadelphia, Pennsylvania on April 9, 1879. He was famous for saying things like, "Anybody who hates children and dogs can't be all bad," "I love children — parboiled," and "I never met a kid I liked." He had a huge nose, always wore a top hat, and talked in an unusual way — out of the side of his mouth. He starred in many movies in the 1920s, 1930s, and 1940s, including *So's Your Old Man*, *My Little Chickadee*, and *Never Give a Sucker an Even*

Break. He was known as W. C. Fields.

✏️ **Who is the grouchiest person you know? What kinds of grouchy things does he or she do? Are you ever grouchy? When do you get grouchy, and why?**

OCTOBER 16

A lexicographer is a person who writes or compiles a dictionary. One of the most famous lexicographers of all time was Noah Webster, who was born on this date in 1758. He was responsible for the first American dictionary, called *An American Dictionary of the English Language*. Webster worked on his dictionary for 25 years — a quarter of a century.

✏️ **Young people often invent new words or new meanings for existing words to use among their friends. They develop a private "language." Write about the language you**

share with your friends. List the latest words and meanings.

OCTOBER 17

You may never have heard of Robert Craig, but you probably know the name he goes by: Evel Knievel. Evel became famous as a daredevil motorcycle stunt performer. His career lasted 16 years, three and a half of them spent in hospitals. He broke 50 or 60 bones and had 14 operations to put steel rods in his body. Robert Craig — Evel Knievel — was born on this date in 1938.

✏️ **Some people like to do dangerous things. Some people have different ideas of what "dangerous" means. Write about something you think is dangerous. Do you think you will ever try it? Why or why not?**

OCTOBER 18

The third Saturday in October is Sweetest Day. People who observe this day try to do a

kind act or remember someone who has done a kind act.

Sweetest Day began sometime in the 1940s in Cleveland, Ohio. A man (his name has been forgotten) started to spread cheer to sick, old, and orphaned people in that city by taking them gifts on the third Saturday in October. Since then, the idea behind Sweetest Day — "a thoughtful word or deed enriches life" — has caught on in other parts of the country, too. Why not celebrate this day yourself?

✏️ **Write about a kind act you have done. Or write about a kind act that someone you know has done. (Maybe it's something he or she did for you.)**

OCTOBER 19

October is National Quality Month. Businesses all over the country are working to improve the quality of their products or services.

✏️ **Have you ever received a poor-quality product or service? (For example, maybe you bought** a radio that fell apart. Or maybe you took your bike in to be fixed and it came back in worse shape than before.) Tell how you felt and what you did.

OCTOBER 20

John Dewey was born on this day in 1859 in Burlington, Vermont. He was an American educator who felt that young people should "learn by doing." He strongly disagreed with authoritarian teaching methods and felt that rote learning — memorization — was a waste of time. Instead, Dewey believed that students should attend laboratory and workshop classes and learn practical things. He felt that classes and studies should be related to students' own interests and problems.

Dewey taught at several universities during his lifetime and became known throughout the world. He died on June 1, 1952, in New York City.

✏️ **How do you learn best? By listening, by reading, or by "doing"? Write about a time when you learned something by "doing" it. (For example, you didn't learn how to ride a bicycle by looking at pictures in a book!)**

OCTOBER 21

This is Edison Lamp Day, also called the Electric Incandecent Lamp Anniversary, in honor of Thomas A. Edison. He invented the first electric light in his Menlo Park, New Jersey, laboratory in 1879. (For more about Edison, see pages 26-27, February 11 entry.)

✏️ **How would the world be different if there were no electric lights? How would your life be different?**

OCTOBER 22

The last full week in October is National Cleaner Air Week.

Air pollution has become a serious concern in recent years. It has been shown to affect weather, climate, and rainfall patterns, even the quality of the sunlight that reaches the earth. Maybe you have heard about the "greenhouse effect" — a gradual increase in the Earth's temperature caused by air pollution. It is estimated that air pollution costs $16 billion a year in the United States alone.

Chemicals that pollute the air include chlorofluorocarbons,

which are used in air conditioners and other appliances, and spray-can propellants, which destroy ozone in the atmosphere. (The ozone layer protects the Earth from dangerous ultraviolet radiation.) Automobile exhaust is another big problem. Plants and trees won't grow along some highways because of the high levels of automobile exhaust.

If you would like more information about air pollution, write to:

Air Pollution Control League
18 E. Fourth Street, Room 211
Cincinnati, Ohio 45202

✎ **Does the weather where you live seem warmer than it used to be? Has air pollution caused any problems for you personally? What is your opinion on the causes of air pollution? Is there anything you can do to help?**

OCTOBER 23

Late-night talk-show host Johnny Carson was born on this date in 1925. Probably in his honor, today is TV Talk Show Host Day.

✎ **What do you do on nights when you get to stay up extra late? Watch TV?**

Read? Work on hobbies or special projects? Write about how you spend your time.

OCTOBER 24

The roller skate was invented by Joseph Merlin, a Belgian, in about 1760. The first patent for a roller skate went to a Frenchman named Petitbled. An American, James Plimpton, refined the skate in 1863 and organized the New York Roller Skating Association. Plimpton also opened the first roller rink, in New York City.

Competitive speed skating began in 1937. In 1979, roller skating competitions were made part of the Pan American Games. Someday roller skating may become an Olympic sport.

Why all this information about roller skating? Because October is National Roller Skating Month. Even though October is almost over, there's still time for you do some skating!

✎ **Do you roller skate? Which do you like better, regular skates or Rollerblades? Write about your roller skating. If you don't roller skate, write about why you think skating has become such a popular recreational activity.**

OCTOBER 25

Today begins Peace, Friendship, and Good Will week. This week occurs every year between October 25 and October 31. Its purpose is to draw attention to the need for peace and good will all over the world. It promotes international friendship and understanding. If you would like more information about Peace, Friendship, and Good Will week, write to:

International Society of
Friendship and Good Will
Dr. Stanley Drake, President
Box 2637
Gastonia, North Carolina
28503-2637

✎ **Write about your best friend. Describe him or her and tell what the two of you like about each other. Or tell about things you like to do together.**

OCTOBER 26

National Pie Day falls on or near this date each year. There are so many kinds of pies that you could eat a different kind every day for more than a month!

✎ **Write about your favorite pie. Do you eat it plain or à la mode (with ice cream)? Is it better warm or cold? Is there a kind of pie you haven't tried that you would like to try someday?**

OCTOBER 27

Theodore Roosevelt performed a number of Presidential firsts. He was the first President to ride in a car, to go undersea in a submarine, and to fly in an airplane. The Teddy Bear is supposedly named after him.

✎ **Why do you think so many people like Teddy Bears? Not just kids — many adults collect them. Write about a Teddy Bear. It can be one you own or have seen, one that someone else owns, or one you would like to have someday.**

OCTOBER 28

This is the Statue of Liberty's birthday. (No, she wasn't "born" on the Fourth of July.) The famous sculpture by Frederic Auguste Bartholdi was dedicated on this day in 1886 in a ceremony presided over by President Grover Cleveland.

"Miss Liberty" was a gift from France. She arrived in the United States in June 1885, in 214 packing cases. She weighs 225 tons. From her heel to the top of her head, she measures 111 feet 1 inch. Her index finger is 8 feet long, and her nose is 4 feet 6 inches long. Her mouth is 3 feet wide. And her full name is "Liberty Enlightening the World."

✎ **Write about what you did on the Fourth of July. Describe all the sights, sounds, and smells you can remember. If the weather is turning a little chilly where you live, this might help you feel warmer!**

OCTOBER 29

This is National Magic Week. October 31 — two days from today — is National Magic Day to honor the death of Harry Houdini, one of America's greatest magicians. Houdini was born on March 24, 1874 and died on Halloween in 1926.

Would you like to know something about magic? Here are some facts to get you started.

There are basically five kinds of magic. "Sleight-of-hand" magic has been around since the days of ancient Egypt. "Close-up" magic is done with the audience very close to the magician. "Illusions" magic makes use of animals, fancy equipment, and often a human assistant. (The most famous illusion is the one in which a person is sawed in half.) In "Escape" magic, the magician escapes from some predicament. (Houdini was a famous escape artist.) Finally, "Mentalist" magic involves mind-reading tricks and predictions.

The two largest magic organizations in the United States today are the Society of American Magicians (S.A.M.) and the International Brotherhood of Magicians (I.B.M.). You can write to them at their headquarters:

S.A.M.
66 Marked Tree Road
Needham, Massachusetts
02192

I.B.M.
114 N. Detroit Street
Kenton, Ohio 43326

If you would like more information about National Magic Week, write to:

Society of American
Magicians, Inc.
Anthony D. Murphy, Esquire
11 Angel Road
North Reading, Maryland
01864

 Describe a magic trick you have seen. Try to explain how the trick worked. If you have no idea how the trick worked, tell why you found it interesting enough to watch.

OCTOBER 30

On this date in 1888, John J. Loud of Massachusetts received a patent for a pen "having a spheroidal marking-point capable of revolving in all directions." In other words, Loud had invented the ballpoint pen.

 Pens used to be made of feathers (quills) sharpened and dipped into ink. Write about how ballpoints have changed things. (For example: You can carry a ballpoint in your pocket, which means you don't ever have to be without something to write with.)

OCTOBER 31

Wandering through a haunted house is fun to do on Halloween. Dressing up in costumes, having parties, and trick-or-treating are more fun things people like to do on the "spookiest" night of the year.

 Describe your favorite costume, from this year or the past. Or describe the costume you would like to wear tonight if you could be anyone (or anything!) you wanted.

NOVEMBER 1

Authors' Day has been observed on this day since 1928, when a woman named Nellie Verne Burt McPherson started it. McPherson's reasons were patriotic. She thought there should be a day to recognize the loyalty and patriotism of American authors, and to encourage people to write things that would support a better America. Today we just honor authors.

✎ **If you were an author, what kind of book would you write? Would it be a mystery, a how-to book, a horror story, a romance, a science-fiction adventure, a fantasy, or a collection of short stories? Why would you write this kind of book?**

NOVEMBER 2

Daniel Boone was born on this day in 1734. He was an explorer and frontiersman who continued hunting well into his 80s. The Shawnee Indians called him "Big Turtle." Boone died in Missouri in 1820.

✎ **You have probably heard some of the "tall tales" told about Daniel Boone. Why do you think the Shawnee called him "Big Turtle"? If you like, you may create your own "tall tale" to answer this question.**

NOVEMBER 3

John Montague, the Fourth Earl of Sandwich, was born on November 3, 1718. The Earl was a gambler who liked to play cards. But he didn't like having to stop for meals. So he invented the sandwich so he could eat and play at the same time.

✎ **What is your favorite sandwich? Write a recipe giving the exact directions for making your sandwich. Start by listing the ingredients, then tell how you put them all together.**

135

NOVEMBER 4

William Penn Adair Rogers was born in Oklahoma Territory on this date in 1879. Will Rogers was an American humorist and author who became known as the "cowboy philosopher." His social and political comments made him very popular. He said things like, "We can't all be heroes because somebody has to sit on the curb and clap as they go by." And "I don't make jokes. I just watch the government and report the facts." And "My folks didn't come over on the Mayflower, but they were there to meet the boat." (Rogers had Indian ancestors.)

✎ **A philosopher is a person who thinks deeply and searches for wisdom. Philosophy is the study of why people think what they think and do what they do. What is your "philosophy" about school? Write a thoughtful, wise statement.**

NOVEMBER 5

This is the anniversary of the Gunpowder Plot in Great Britain. In 1605, 11 men planned to blow up the Houses of Parliament and King James I. Twenty barrels of gunpowder were smuggled into the basement under Parliament, with plans to explode them on November 5, but they were discovered on the night of November 4. The 11 men, including one named Guy Fawkes, were arrested, tried, and beheaded. In Great Britain today, people celebrate "mischief night" on November 4 with bonfires and firecrackers.

✎ **Think of a time when you were very mischievous. Tell what you did and what happened as a result.**

NOVEMBER 6

James Naismith was born in Canada on this date in 1861. In 1891, Dr. Naismith originated the game of basketball. In 1936, basketball became part of the Olympic Games. The National Basketball Association was established in 1949. It is said that Dr. Naismith created the game as a class assignment.

✎ **What is the most creative class assignment a teacher ever gave you? (Think back to past years, too.) Tell about the assignment and why you enjoyed** doing it. If you can't remember ever getting a creative assignment, write about an assignment you would like to do someday.

NOVEMBER 7

Marie Sklodowska Curie was the first woman to receive the Nobel Prize. In fact, she won it twice! She won her first Nobel in physics in 1903, and her second Nobel in chemistry in 1911. She was born in Poland on November 7, 1867 and died on July 4, 1934.

✏️ **Many people feel that science is a "man's field" — that men are better at science than women, and women shouldn't even try to be scientists. What is your opinion? Give your reasons for feeling the way you do.**

NOVEMBER 8

Edmund Halley became a famous astronomer after he observed a comet in 1682. He studied many old records and predicted that the comet would return in the year 1758. Halley didn't live to see his prediction come true — he died in 1742 — but the comet was named after him anyway. Halley's Comet did return in 1758 and continues to return about every 76 years. The first recorded appearance was in 240 B.C., and there have been 28 return appearances since then. Halley was born in London on this date in 1656.

✏️ **There is a good chance that you will still be alive when Halley's Comet returns in the year 2062. Write as if it is 2062 now, and you are waiting to see the comet. Tell something about your life in the 21st century.**

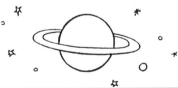

NOVEMBER 9

A statue called "Three Servicemen" was unveiled in Washington, D.C. on this date in 1984. This statue faces the Wall, the black granite memorial to the Vietnam War that bears the names of the 58,000 Americans who lost their lives in that conflict.

The Wall was designed by Maya Ying Lin, a Chinese-American. She was a 22-year-old architecture student at Yale University when she entered her design into a competition. There were 1,420 other entries, but hers won.

The Wall actually has two angled walls, each 250 feet long, that meet in the center. Each slopes from a height of 10 feet down to ground level. The names of the Americans who died in the Vietnam War are carved into the Wall and arranged in order, starting with the first who died in 1959 and ending with the last who died in 1975. It was dedicated on November 13, 1982.

✎ **If you have not visited the Vietnam Veterans Memorial and seen the Wall in person, you have probably seen pictures of it. Write your reaction to the Wall.**

NOVEMBER 10

Book Week was first observed starting on this date in 1919. Now National Children's Book Week is celebrated every year around this time. If you would like more information about National Children's Book Week, write to:

> The Children's Book
> Council, Inc.
> Publicity Department
> 67 Irving Place
> New York, New York 10003

✎ **Write about your favorite children's book. Give the title and the author's name, then tell what the book is about.**

NOVEMBER 11

On the eleventh hour of the eleventh day of the eleventh month of 1919, a silent memorial was observed for the Armistice of World War One. This day used to be called Armistice Day for that reason. In 1954, Armistice Day was officially renamed Veterans' Day. From 1971–1978, Veterans' Day was observed on the fourth Monday of November. In 1978, it was changed back to November 11, and that is when we observe it today. In some places, Veterans' Day is called Remembrance Day or Victory Day.

✎ **Remember someone. The person does not have to be a soldier, but should be someone who is no longer around for one reason or another. (He or she can even be a friend who moved away.) Give the person's name and reasons why you remember him or her. Tell what made that person special to you.**

NOVEMBER 12

On this date in 1981, the space shuttle *Columbia* was launched from Cape Kennedy (now Cape Canaveral) in Florida. The astronauts aboard were Joe Engle and Richard Truly. *Columbia* was the first space shuttle — the first spacecraft designed to return to Earth and be launched again.

✎ **Write your feelings about the space shuttle disaster that occurred on Jan-**

uary 28, 1986, when the *Challenger* exploded. (If you need to refresh your memory about that event, see page 21, January 28 entry.)

NOVEMBER 13

Robert Louis Stevenson was born on this date in Scotland in 1850. In 1883, he wrote a famous adventure novel called *Treasure Island*. In 1886, he wrote *Kidnapped* and *The Strange Case of Dr. Jekyll and Mr. Hyde*. Stevenson wrote a number of other books, but these three have remained his most famous.

✎ **Write about an adventure you once had or were part of. Tell where you were, who you were with, and what you did.**

NOVEMBER 14

Today is the anniversary of the first blood transfusion, which was done in 1666. This important medical breakthrough was recorded in the Diary of Samuel Pepys. (For more about this Diary, see page 31, February 23 entry.)

✎ There have been many changes in medical treatment since 1666. Describe some medical breakthroughs you would like to see happen in the next 50 years.

NOVEMBER 15

Shichi-Go-San means "seven-five-three" in Japan. Today that country is celebrating its seven-year-olds, five-year-olds, and three-year-olds. Many years ago, in old Japan, children often did not live very long. Shichi-Go-San became a special time for parents and their children.

✎ Write about what you remember of your life when you were three, five, or seven years old.

NOVEMBER 16

William Christopher Handy, known as W. C. Handy, was born on this day in 1873. He was an African-American songwriter and bandleader whom many consider to be the "Father of the Blues."

✎ Rap music is as popular today as the Blues were

a few years ago. What are your feelings on Rap? Do you have a favorite Rap group? If yes, tell the name of the group and why you like their music.

NOVEMBER 17

Do you like the smell of bread baking in your kitchen at home? Then you'll appreciate that today is Homemade Bread Day.

Relatively few people today still make bread from scratch. It can be an all-day project. The flour and yeast and other ingredients are mixed and left to rest. The dough is kneaded, left to expand, and sometimes kneaded again. Then it is shaped into loaves, baked, and put on racks to cool. Many people do not have time to prepare homemade bread — but we all have time to eat it!

If you would like more information about Homemade Bread Day, write to:

Homemade Bread Day
Committee
Box 26
Montague, Michigan 49437

✎ Write about an all-day (or almost all-day) project you did around your home. Maybe you cleaned the basement or your closet. Maybe you helped to build something. Maybe you even baked bread!

NOVEMBER 18

On this day in 1928, Mickey Mouse made his first on-screen appearance. He starred in a Walt Disney film called *Steamboat Willie* that was shown at the Colony Theatre in New York City. *Steamboat Willie* was the first talking animated cartoon picture.

✎ Write about your favorite animated cartoon. It can be one you saw in a movie theater, or one you saw on TV at home. Give the names of the characters, describe some of the things that happened, and tell why this cartoon is your favorite.

NOVEMBER 19

On November 19, 1863, President Abraham Lincoln went to Gettysburg, Pennsylvania, for the dedication of a Civil War cemetery. He made a speech that began, "Four score and seven years ago..." Lincoln's speech lasted less than three minutes, yet it became very

famous. It is said that the Gettysburg Address is the most-quoted speech of all time. (For more about Abraham Lincoln, see page 27, February 12 entry.)

✎ Abraham Lincoln is considered to be one of America's greatest Presidents. Why? Write about his life and some of the things he did to become a great President. Or, if you know more about another President than you do about Lincoln, write about him instead.

NOVEMBER 20

Selma Lagerlöf was the first woman to receive the Nobel Prize for Literature in 1909. Born on November 20, 1858, she was a Swedish novelist who based her books on stories she had heard as a child. One of her books, *The Wonderful Adventures of Nils*, is a children's classic. It is the story of a tiny boy who flies on the back of a goose and has adventures all around Sweden. Lagerlöf died on March 16, 1940.

✎ Special effects in movies can make people seem very small and everyday objects seem very large. (If you have seen the movie called *Honey, I Shrunk the Kids,* then you know what this is like!) Pretend that you are only half an inch tall. Pick an everyday object and describe it from your new perspective.

NOVEMBER 21

In Paris on this day in 1783, Jean Francois Pilatre de Rozier and the Marquis Francois Laurent d'Arlandes became the first men to fly in a hot-air balloon. This happened only a year after the Montgolfier brothers, Joseph and Jacques, had done their first experiments with small paper and fabric balloons at Annonay, France.

✎ Pretend that you are in a hot-air balloon race. Describe the sights, smells, and sounds. (If you have never been in a hot-air balloon, you may not be aware that it's very quiet when the burner isn't firing. You can even hear things that are happening on the ground below you.)

NOVEMBER 22

President John Fitzgerald Kennedy, the youngest man ever to hold the office of President of the United States, was assassinated on this day in 1963. He was riding in a motorcade in Dallas, Texas when he was shot and killed. A man named Lee Harvey Oswald was arrested and charged with the murder.

On November 24, two days later, Oswald was shot and killed by Dallas nightclub owner Jack Ruby. Oswald was being moved from one holding area to another, and TV cameras were filming the transfer. Viewers all over the world saw Ruby shoot Oswald.

Ruby was convicted of murder on March 14, 1964. He was sentenced to death. While waiting for a retrial, he died of natural causes on January 3, 1967.

✎ What do you think of live-action, on-the-scene TV reporting? Many people today believe that TV cameras don't just record the news, but also "make it happen." For example, a demonstration doesn't start until the TV crews arrive. Or people "act out" and do things they wouldn't do if the cameras weren't around. Write your feelings about this issue. Do you think that people have the right to see this kind of TV reporting? Why or why not?

NOVEMBER 23

He was a legendary outlaw of the Old West, but no one is sure what his real name was. Some people believe that he was born Henry McCarty on this date in 1859 in New York City. Others think that his name was William H. Bonney. He was known as Billy the Kid.

The Kid was a large-scale cattle rustler and cold-blooded killer. On July 15, 1881, he was shot by Patrick F. Garrett, a county sheriff and former friend of Billy's. Many stories have since been told about the Kid's life — and most have proved to be untrue.

Cowboy movies and television shows have been around for a long time. Books about cowboys are popular, and cowboy clothes go in and out of fashion. Why do you think

people are so fascinated by cowboys? Would you have wanted to be a cowboy in the days of the Wild West? Why or why not?

NOVEMBER 24

On November 24, 1971, a middle-aged man called D. B. Cooper threatened to blow up a Northwest Airlines 727 jet he was riding on. He allowed the pilot to land the plane long enough to exchange the passengers for $200,000 in ransom money — 10,000 $20 bills. Then the plane took off again with Cooper on board.

Authorities had not planned on what happened next. Somewhere over the snowy Cascade Mountains near Ariel, Washington, Cooper parachuted out of the plane. He had the $200,000 in his backpack. He parachuted into a wilderness area in the middle of a storm.

In February of 1980, almost ten years later, about 300 of the bills used to pay the ransom were found, wet and shredded, along the Columbia River near Vancouver, Washington. The rest of the money has never turned up in circulation, meaning that it probably hasn't been spent. And D. B. Cooper has never been heard from again.

✎ **What do you think might have happened to D. B. Cooper? Did he get away with his crime, or did something else happen to him? Write an ending to his story as though you know all of the details. Make it believable! (In other words, please don't write about Cooper being rescued by aliens and taken to another planet.)**

NOVEMBER 25

Before the year 1973, many people drove 70 miles per hour without breaking the law. But on this date in 1973, a law was passed to lower the speed limit to 55 miles per hour. The law would take effect in 1974, giving the states time to make new road signs.

During the 1970s, the United States was going through an "energy crisis." States were told that they would lose Federal money if they didn't enforce the new speed limit. In fact, it saved lives, reduced the number of highway-related injuries, and saved up to 2.4 billion gallons of fuel per year.

Meanwhile, people complained, especially in the Western states. They said that because of the speed limit, it took too long to get places. In 1987, the Senate voted to allow states to raise speed limits to 65 miles per hour on stretches of rural interstate highways. Each state can decide for itself whether it wants to do this.

✎ **On German autobahns (special roads that are something like American freeways), there is no speed limit, except near cities or construction areas. People can drive as fast as they want — 55, or 155! Do you think that drivers in the United States should be able to go that fast? Explain your answer.**

NOVEMBER 26

In 1789, President George Washington proclaimed that the first national Thanksgiving Day would be held on November 26. Meanwhile the Protestant Episcopal Church announced that the first Thursday in November would be a good time to give thanks each year. Most people ignored both dates until 1863, when President Abraham Lincoln proposed that Thanksgiving be celebrated on the last Thursday in November. Every year after that, for 75 years, Presidents made formal proclamations following Lincoln's lead.

In 1939, President Franklin D. Roosevelt moved Thanksgiving Day one week backward. He did it to help businesses. People usually didn't start their Christmas shopping until after Thanksgiving, and Roosevelt's change made the shopping season a week longer.

✐ **List three things from this year that you are thankful for. Tell about them and why you are thankful for them.**

NOVEMBER 27

The fourth Monday in November is a special day in Berne, Switzerland. It is the beginning of a celebration called Zybelemärit, or "Onion Market."

Zybelemärit dates back to 1405. In that year, there was a devastating fire in the city of Berne. The farmers from the surrounding area came into the city to help rebuild it. In gratitude, the city leaders let the farmers open a Farmers' Market in Berne. Many of the farmers sold strings of onions in their stalls.

During Zybelemärit, a Parade of Onions is held, and onions are piled high in front of the Federal Palace building.

✐ **What is your favorite way to eat onions? Do you slice them raw for hamburgers? Do you dice them and cook them in omelets? Do you eat them on pizza? Write about how you like your onions best. If you don't like onions at all, write about another favorite food.**

NOVEMBER 28

Today marks the birthday of Jean Baptiste Lully in 1632. Lully was born in Italy, but he was known as a French operatic composer because he spent his life in France. He was also known as a man with a very bad temper. He often threw tantrums to vent his anger. During one such tantrum, he punctured his foot with his conducting baton. The puncture wound turned into blood poisoning, which caused Lully's death in 1687.

✎ **Describe a time when you lost your temper. What happened? Why were you angry in the first place? What were the results of your "temper tantrum"?**

NOVEMBER 29

Louisa May Alcott was born in Germantown, Pennsylvania, on this date in 1832. She was a student of poet Ralph Waldo Emerson and author Henry David Thoreau, who were friends of her family.

During the Civil War, Alcott worked as a nurse in a Union hospital. The letters she wrote to her family were published in 1863 under the title *Hospital Sketches*. *Little Women* was published in 1868. Based on her childhood and family life, it was translated into several languages and made her famous around the world.

Alcott wrote several more novels, including *Little Men* and *Jo's Boys*. She died on March 6, 1888.

✎ **Imagine that you are about to write a story based on your family life. Who will be the main character? What is one event you will definitely write about?**

NOVEMBER 30

Samuel Langhorne Clemens was born on this day in 1835, a year in which Halley's Comet was seen. (For more about Halley's Comet, see page 137, November 8 entry.) Clemens was a printer, a newspaper writer, and a river pilot. Using the pseudonym Mark Twain, he also wrote many short stories and novels and became a popular lecturer and humorist. His first successful story was "The Celebrated Jumping Frog of Calaveras County." Twain also wrote *The Adventures of Tom Sawyer* and *The Adventures of Huckleberry Finn*.

Twain was one of the first authors to use dialects, or vernacular speech, in his books.

He spelled words the way they sounded when people said them, not necessarily the way they were supposed to be spelled. Because of this, the characters in his books seem especially realistic.

Twain often said that since he had been born in the year the Comet came, he would die when it returned. And he did — on April 21, 1910.

✎ **Think of some different accents you have heard. Pick one and write a paragraph using that accent. Spell words the way they sound to you when someone with that accent says them aloud.**

DECEMBER 1

On this date in 1955, Mrs. Rosa Parks, a black seamstress in Montgomery, Alabama, got on a bus to ride home from work. She was tired, and her feet hurt. There were no seats available at the back of the bus, where black people were supposed to sit. So she sat down in the front part of the bus. When a white man asked her to get up and move, she decided that her feet hurt too badly. She refused to move. The bus driver drove the bus to the police station, where Rosa Parks was arrested.

This was the beginning of the civil rights movement. Black people in Montgomery boycotted the buses for more than a year after her arrest. After the boycott, racial segregation on city buses was outlawed.

✏️ **Pretend that you are Rosa Parks. You have worked all day, and you are tired. The law says that you must sit in the back of the bus, but all those seats are taken. What will you do? Will you break the law? Why or why not?**

DECEMBER 2

On this day in 1804, at the Cathedral of Notre Dame in Paris, Pope Pius VII raised a crown to place it on a man's head. The man grabbed it and crowned himself.

His name was Napoleon, and he was the most important figure in European history until 1815. A brilliant military leader, he conquered much of western and central Europe and remained in power until 1815, when he lost an important battle with England and Prussia. (For more about this battle, see pages 76–77, June 18 entry.) He died on May 5, 1821.

Napoleon was a "giant among men" — an inspirational, strong, and dramatic leader. He was 5 feet 2 inches tall.

✏️ **Do you think it matters if a person is tall, short, or average in height? Explain your answer.**

DECEMBER 3

This is Heart Transplant Day. On December 3, 1967, in Cape Town, South Africa, Dr. Christiaan Barnard performed the first human heart transplant. The person who got the heart was a man named Louis Washkansky. He lived for 18 days following the operation.

Today over 1,700 heart transplants are performed each year in the United States, and over 2,600 in the world. Many people have lived for several years after surgery. In 1989, some 90 percent of all heart transplant patients were living for longer than a year. The five-year survival rate was 73 percent; the ten-year survival rate was 71½ percent.

✎ **What if you found out that you only had a short time to live? What would you do?**

DECEMBER 4

Edith Louisa Cavell was born on this day in 1865. She was an English nurse who working in a hospital in Brussels, Belgium during World War I. She became a heroine for helping

Allied prisoners. When the Germans found out what she was doing, Cavell was executed by a firing squad.

✎ **Write about someone who is a heroine or hero in your opinion. (This does not have to be a famous person.) What makes you think so highly of this person? What has he or she done?**

DECEMBER 5

Walter Elias Disney was born on this date in 1901 in Chicago, Illinois. After World War I, where he drove a Red Cross truck in France and Germany, he started a small film studio. In 1928, he created Mickey Mouse and the rest is history!

The Disney Studios have pioneered many new trends in filmmaking, cartooning, and amusement parks. Disneyland opened in 1955 in Anaheim, California; Walt Disney World opened in 1971 in Orlando, Florida. Epcot Center in Walt Disney World opened in 1982, followed by Disney-MGM Studios in 1989. There is even a Disneyland in Tokyo, Japan.

✎ **If you could visit any Disney amusement park of your choice, anywhere in the world, which one would you visit and why?**

DECEMBER 6

Alfred Joyce Kilmer was born in New Brunswick, New Jersey, on December 6, 1886. He was killed during World War I, in 1918. Kilmer is best known for his poem, "Trees," which begins, "I think that I shall never see/A poem lovely as a tree." You may want to look up this poem and read it for yourself.

 Write about your favorite tree. If you like, you can write a poem, rhyming or not. Or write a paragraph. Or a letter to the tree. Or a letter to someone else about the tree. Let your imagination go.

DECEMBER 7

You may have heard of Madame Tussaud's Wax Museum, but you probably don't know the story of how it got started. Madame Tussaud was imprisoned in France during the French Revolution, a time when many people were decapitated (meaning that their heads were cut off). This included many famous people. Using their heads as models, Tussaud started crafting heads in wax. Later in life, she inherited a wax museum from her uncle, J.C. Curtius. Several of Tussaud's wax figures are still in the wax museum in London that is named after her. She died in 1850; she was born on this date in 1761.

Many people visit Madame Tussaud's Wax Museum every year. Why do you think the wax figures are so popular? What person (famous or not) would you like to see made into a wax figure?

DECEMBER 8

Jean Sibelius was a Finnish composer and patriot. Most of his works were inspired by his feelings about the forests, lakes, and seasons of his native country.

"Finlandia," his most famous work, was first performed in Helsinki, Finland, in 1900. This musical "tone poem" expressed so much national pride that the Russians, who ruled Finland until 1918, made a rule that it could not be performed again. But the Finns did it anyway — under different titles, to keep the Russians from stopping the performances.

"Finlandia" became the Finnish anthem of independence.

Sibelius was born on this day in 1865. He died on September 20, 1957.

 Many people have emotional reactions to music. They listen to a symphony, an opera, or a single song and it makes them have strong feelings. People feel happy or sad, excited or calm, angry or patriotic — music can cause many different feelings. Have you ever had this kind of experience? Is there a particular piece of music that makes you feel a certain way? Does it bring back memories of a certain time, place, event, or person? Write about your own experience of being "moved" by music. If this has never happened to you, write about your favorite kind of music and tell why it's important to you.

DECEMBER 9

Clarence Birdseye was born on this day in 1886. Birdseye was the founder of the frozen-food industry. He established General Foods Company in 1924, and he developed a process for freezing fish in 1925.

 Write about your favorite frozen food (NOT including pizza). Do you like veggies, fancy noodles, fish sticks, or frozen fruit pies? Tell when you eat your favorite frozen food, what you like to eat with it, and who you like to share it with.

DECEMBER 10

Today is Nobel Prize Presentation Day in honor of Alfred Bernard Nobel, who died on this date in 1896. The awards for achievement in physics, chemistry, medicine, literature, and economics are given in Stockholm, Sweden. The Nobel Peace Prize is presented in Oslo, Norway. The winners each receive a gold medal and anywhere from $150,000 to $300,000. The first Nobel awards were given in 1901.

Nobel established a fund for the awards in his will. Also in his will, he specified that the awards must go to those individuals who have done the most to contribute to the good of humanity.

The Nobel Peace Prize may have been the result of a guilty conscience. Alfred Nobel invented dynamite in 1866, and it made him very rich. Later he had terrible guilt feelings for creating something that caused so much injury and death. He hated the fact that dynamite — which he had invented for peace — could be used in war. The Peace Prize may have been his way to make up for that.

✎ **Do you think that the Nobel Peace Prize makes up for the fact that Nobel invented dynamite? Explain your answer. Or write a response to this question: Is it possible to "cancel out" bad with good? If yes, give an example you know about.**

DECEMBER 11

Edward Albert Christian George Andrew Patrick David, better known as King Edward VIII, became king of England in January of 1936. On December 11, less than a year later, he abdicated (gave up) his throne. King Edward had fallen in love with an American woman named Wallis can woman named Wallis Warfield Simpson who had already been married and divorced twice. When he was told that he could not marry her and remain King, he became an "ordinary" citizen so he could marry the woman he loved. Edward died on May 28, 1972.

✎ **Imagine that it's 1936 and you are a British citizen. You have just heard the news: the King has abdicated his throne! You have also learned the reason why. Write your reactions.**

DECEMBER 12

On this date in 1792, Ludwig van Beethoven paid the equivalent of 19 cents for his first music lesson. His teacher was Franz Joseph Haydn. Haydn was a friend of Wolfgang Amadeus Mozart, and the two of them shared many musical ideas.

Beethoven, Haydn, and Mozart are considered to be three of the greatest composers of all time. People all over the world still perform, listen to, and study their works.

✎ **Have you ever taken special lessons of any kind — music, tennis, art, dance, language, swimming, or anything else? If yes, write about your lessons. How** long did you take them? Who was your teacher? If no, tell what kind of lessons you would like to take someday.

DECEMBER 13

The is Santa Lucia Day in Sweden. It is a time for celebrating and thanking Saint Lucia, the Queen of Light, for returning after the darkness of winter.

Part of Sweden is located inside the Arctic Circle, an area often called "The Land of the Midnight Sun" because the sun shines 24 hours a day during certain parts of the summer. In the winter, the sun does not rise at all for several weeks.

In some families, on Santa Lucia Day, the oldest daughter serves breakfast to the other family members while wearing a crown of lighted candles.

✎ **What do members of your family do to "treat" one another? Write about at least one special and loving thing they do just to be nice.**

DECEMBER 14

Michel de Notredame was born on this day in 1503 in St. Remy, France. He was a physician, but he is best remembered for writing predictions for the future in rhymed quatrains, a special type of poetry. He wrote under the name Nostradamus, the Latin spelling of Notredame. He died in 1566, but many of his predictions lived on after him. Some people today believe that they reached all the way into our time and beyond — that some of Nostradamus's predictions haven't come true yet, but will.

✎ **Predict something. Anything. Tell what you think will happen, where you think it will happen, and who will be involved. You don't have to write a serious entry. For example, you may want to predict that your little brother Alphonse will stop bugging you someday.**

DECEMBER 15

Alexandre Gustave Eiffel was born on this date in 1832. He was a French engineer who designed the Eiffel Tower in France. He also helped to design the Statue of Liberty, a gift from France to the United States. The Eiffel Tower is 984 feet high and weighs more than 7,000 tons. Many people travel to Paris every year to see it.

✎ **Have you ever visited a famous monument? If yes, write about it. If no, write about a monument you would like to visit someday, and tell why you would like to go there.**

DECEMBER 16

Records show that the weather is usually very calm for seven days before and after the Winter Solstice, which falls on or about December 21. In ancient times, people made up stories to explain this natural occurrence. Here is one story from long ago.

The ancient Greeks called the kingfisher bird a "halcyon." They believed that the halcyon built its nest on the ocean's surface and had the ability to quiet the wind so its eggs could hatch safely. According to legend, it was the halcyon that caused the two-week period of calm around the Winter Solstice.

Some of this story lives on in our modern language. Today we use the term "Halcyon Days" to describe any time of peace and prosperity.

✎ **Pretend that you are an ancient witnessing a natural occurrence. For example, you might be "seeing" a tornado, the tide rising, the Northern Lights, a flock of geese flying south, a volcanic eruption, a total eclipse of the moon — anything you can think of! Now make up a story to explain what you "see." (Do not give the real reason it happens, even if you know it.)**

DECEMBER 17

Sometime around 1892, two brothers named Orville and Wilbur Wright operated a bicycle shop and experimented with kites and gliders in their spare time. On this day in 1893, one of their inventions made history. It was a self-powered airplane, and the two brothers managed to keep

155

it in the air for almost a minute during one of its first flights.

Wilbur died on May 30, 1912 of typhoid fever. Orville died on January 30, 1948. By that time flying was an ordinary, everyday thing. Planes crossed continents and oceans and circled the globe. Today planes are bigger, faster, and carry more people farther than the Wright Brothers ever dreamed. (For more about the Wright Brothers, see page 102, August 19 entry.)

✎ **Write about another invention that has greatly changed the world. Tell what it is and how you think those changes have affected you personally.**

DECEMBER 18

See if you can guess the name of this game:

Up to eight people can play it at a time. It comes with a pair of dice, special cards, play money, deeds to streets and

utilities in Atlantic City, New Jersey, little houses and hotels made of plastic or wood, and metal playing pieces. To win, you need to gain wealth and property while bankrupting the other players. If your grandparents were Christmas shopping about this time in 1935, they could have purchased one of the first copies ever made.

If you guessed Monopoly®, you're right!

✎ **Describe your favorite game. Tell how you play it and who you play it with, list the most important rules, and explain why this game is your favorite.**

DECEMBER 19

Satellites and satellite transmissions are very common today. Weather, radio, and TV signals are frequently sent by satellite. But it wasn't that long ago that satellites were brand new. The first broadcast from outer space took place on this day in 1958. At 3:15 P.M. EST (Eastern Standard Time), President Dwight David Eisenhower sent a message over the satellite *Atlas*, which had been launched from Cape Canaveral the day before. The President's message was less than 60 words long and ended by sending "to all mankind, America's wish for peace on earth and good will toward men everywhere."

✎ **You have been given two minutes of free time on international television and radio. Write your "script" — what you plan to say to people all over the world.**

DECEMBER 20

Sacagawea, sometimes called Bird Woman, was a Shoshone Indian. She traveled with the Lewis and Clark Expedition that explored the Louisiana Purchase and beyond to the Pacific Ocean. She served as a guide across the Rockies and as an interpreter throughout the trip. Just before the expedition began, she gave birth to a baby boy. She carried him on her back during her travels. It is said that Sacagawea lived to be almost 100 years old. She died on this date in 1812.

✎ **How old would you like to live to be? What are some of the things you hope to accomplish during your lifetime?**

DECEMBER 21

"I will bet twenty thousand pounds...that I will make the tour of the world in eighty days or less." So said Phileas Fogg on October 2, 1872. On December 21, 1872, with only a few seconds to spare, he made a grand entrance into the clubroom where the bet had been made. In front of the amazed members of the club, he announced, "Here I am, gentlemen!" Fogg had gone around the world in 79 days, 23 hours, and 59 minutes!

None of this happened in real life. But all of it (and much more) happened in a book called *Around the World in Eighty Days*. It was written by a Frenchman named Jules Verne and first published in 1873. Your library is sure to have a copy, if you want to read it yourself.

✎ **Have you ever finished something — like a project or a paper — at the very "last minute" before it was due? Have you ever rushed into a movie seconds before it started, or gone anywhere else and arrived just in time? Choose an experience like this** from your own life and write about it. Tell what happened and how you felt before, during, and after.

DECEMBER 22

Chanuka, also spelled Hanukkah, is a word meaning "dedication." Chanuka is the Jewish Festival of Lights. It is celebrated around this time each year to commemorate the rededication of the Temple in Jerusalem by Judas Maccabeus in 165 B.C., more than 2,000 years ago. A special candelabrum called a Menorah is used as part of the Chanuka ceremonies.

✎ **What is your favorite time to use candles? During Chanuka, at Christmas, for holiday family dinners? Write about your favorite time. Or, if you have ever made candles, describe what that was like.**

DECEMBER 23

This is the time of year when the Audubon Christmas Bird Count is held. Each year since 1900, the National Audubon Society has sponsored a bird census. From December 15 to January 2, more than 41,000 birdwatchers in North and Central America count the birds they see. Then they try to estimate how many birds there are altogether. If you would like more information about the Audubon Christmas Bird Count, write to:

The National Audubon Society
950 Third Avenue
New York, New York 10022

✎ **Are you a birdwatcher? If yes, tell what you enjoy most about this popular sport. If no, tell about another animal you like to watch.**

DECEMBER 24

Howard Robard Hughes was born on this day in 1902. He was a wealthy businessman. He was also a pilot who set several aviation records. Plus he produced motion pictures! Hughes became almost a hermit in his later years. He was considered to be quite an eccentric and had unusual personal habits. It is said that he had billions of dollars when he died in 1976.

✎ **What would you do with a billion dollars? Write a detailed account of how you would spend, save, or use this money.**

DECEMBER 25

This is Christmas Day. It is said that the word Christmas is descended from "Cristes Maesse," which meant "the Mass of Christ" back in 1038. Christians believe that Jesus Christ had a lowly birth in a manger in a stable in Bethlehem. This holiday is considered one of the most joyous days of the Christian year.

✎ **Describe something in your life that gives you joy. This can be another person, a thing, an achievement, your faith — anything you choose.**

DECEMBER 26

On this day in 1913, Ambrose Bierce wrote his last letter from somewhere in Mexico and was never heard from again.

Born on June 24, 1842, in Meigs County, Ohio, Bierce was a famous author by the time he disappeared. (Maybe you have read his story, "Occurrence at Owl Creek Bridge.") But he seemed to be tired of life in America when, in 1913, he left for Mexico to look for the rebel leader Pancho Villa. Bierce may have found Villa and his army; nobody knows for sure. It is believed that he died in battle in late 1913 or early 1914.

✎ **Write a letter to someone from long ago. Pick a figure from history — a leader, a writer, an inventor, or anyone else you choose. In your letter, tell something about yourself and your life.**

DECEMBER 27

Louis Pasteur was born on December 27, 1822, in Dole, France. He was a French chemist known for his studies of bacteria. He discovered that bacteria spread diseases and he developed the process of pasteurization, which kills harmful germs in milk. Pasteur also developed vaccines for anthrax and rabies. He proved that vaccinations could be used to prevent various diseases. In 1888 he helped to found the Pasteur Institute, a world center for the study, prevention, and treatment of diseases. He is buried in a tomb in the building.

✎ **Because of Pasteur and those who followed in his footsteps, many diseases are now under control or no longer exist. Food products and medicines are safer to use. Write about a disease that you would like to see brought under control or eliminated. Give your reasons for wanting to rid the world of this disease.**

DECEMBER 28

This is Bingo's Birthday Month. Edwin S. Lowe invented and first manufactured the game of Bingo in 1929. Today churches and other organizations earn billions of dollars for charity each year because of Bingo.

✎ **Write about the last time you played Bingo. What do you like most about the game? What do you like**

least about it? Can you think of any ways to improve it or make it more fun?

DECEMBER 29

Grigori Yefimovich Rasputin was born in Siberia sometime around 1872. Nicholas II was Emperor of Russia, and Alexandra was Empress. Their children had hemophilia, a dangerous condition which prevents blood from clotting. People with hemophilia — called hemophiliacs — can bleed to death if they are cut or injured.

Rasputin was able to control the children's hemophilia, and because of this he became very powerful. He also became very corrupt, even evil. Over time, the name Rasputin has come to stand for corruption and evil. He was murdered on this date in 1916.

✎ **The words "decadent," "abject," "rotten," "villain," "degenerate," "devious," "felonious," "venal," and "scoundrel" can all be used to describe Rasputin.**

Some of these words may not be familiar to you, but they all have similar meanings. What are some words that have opposite meanings? (Some simple examples: good, kind, gentle.) Write about a someone you know who could be described with these words — someone who is good, kind, gentle, …?

DECEMBER 30

Joseph Rudyard Kipling was born in India on this date in 1865. His parents were English. Kipling grew up to be a writer and received the Nobel Prize in literature in 1907. Some of his best-known works include a collection of stories for children called *The Jungle Book* and a poem, "Gunga Din."

"Gunga Din" tells about a brave Indian native who is made fun of because of his color and race and bullied because he is only a lowly water carrier. The narrator, a British soldier, is rescued by Gunga Din at the expense of the water carrier's life. By the end of the poem, the narrator has learned, "You're a better man than I am, Gunga Din!"

✎ As you near the end of the year, write about something important you have learned over the past 12 months. Try to make this a personal statement of how you have grown and changed.

DECEMBER 31

New Year's Eve has been celebrated since at least 46 B.C., when Julius Caesar established New Year's Day. In A.D. 567, the Christian church outlawed the celebration, which was originally dedicated to the Roman god Janus, the god of gates, doors, and beginnings. Pictures and statues of Janus show him with two faces — one looking forward, another looking backward.

The old Roman custom was revived in the 1200s. New Year's Eve became a time when people brought gifts to their rulers. This custom disappeared in the 1800s.

Different groups have celebrated New Year's at different times of the year. In the 1600s, the Gregorian calendar was

adopted, restoring January 1
as New Year's Day. American
colonists used this calendar
starting in 1752. But New
Year's can still be celebrated at
other times. Some religions
dictate when their New Year
begins. Various peoples
around the world have developed their own customs to celebrate a new beginning.

✎ **Is there something
you would like to begin
again — to start over?
Why? What would you do
for your new beginning?**

RESOURCES

Alexander, Rosemary, *Instructor's Page-A-Day Pursuits* (New York, NY: Instructor Books, 1984).

Contains various subject-matter activities for the entire school year. For elementary grades.

Bayne, Sarah, *Helping Kids Write: A Practical Guide for Teaching Children to Express Themselves on Paper* (Cambridge, MA: Educators Publishing Service, Inc., 1980).

Offers some excellent ideas and reinforcement for encouraging writing in the classroom. For grades 5–8.

Calkins, Lucy M., *The Art of Teaching Writing* (Portsmith, NH: Heinemann Educational Books, Inc., 1986).

Chase's Annual Events: Special Days, Weeks and Months in 1989 (Chicago, IL: Contemporary Books, Inc., 1988).

The most up-to-date information on current happenings. Published yearly; a fun resource.

Christian, Barbara, *Creative Escapes: Adventures in Writing for Grades 7–12* (Belmont, CA: Pitman Learning, Inc., 1980).

Creative ideas for the secondary teacher for the instruction of grammar and composition.

Frank, Marjorie, *If You're Going to Teach Kids How to Write, You've Gotta Have This Book!* (Nashville, TN: Incentive Publications, 1979).

The title says it all. Worthwhile in any classroom.

Graves, Donald and Virginia Stuart, *Write from the Start: How to Tap Your Child's Innate Writing Abilities* (New York, NY: New American Library, 1987).

Gregory, Ruth W., *Anniversaries and Holidays* (Chicago, IL: American Library Association, 1975).

Lists "holy days and religious festivals, days which commemorate the lives of famous men and women, civic holidays and special-event days" for every day of the year. Gives more in-depth information on certain dates.

Harwayne, Shelley, *The Writing Workshop: A World of Difference* (Portsmith, NH: Heinemann Educational Books, Inc., 1987).

Hirsch, E.D., Jr., Joseph F. Kett, and James Trefil, *The Dictionary of Cultural Literacy: What Every American Needs to Know* (Boston, MA: Houghton Mifflin Company, 1988).

What fun! Full of great bits of information to expand classroom programs. A wonderful reference guide.

Michener, Dorothy, and Beverly Muschlitz, *Day In Day Out* (Nashville, TN: Incentive Publications, Inc., 1980).

Contains many ideas and worksheets for various holidays. For elementary grades.

Newmann, Dana, *The New Teacher's Almanack* (New York, NY: The Center for Applied Research in Education, Inc., 1980).

Full of historical notes and ideas for the teaching year. Aimed, generally, at the elementary age group.

Rico, Gabriele Lusser, *Writing the Natural Way* (Los Angeles, CA: J.P. Tarcher, Inc., 1983).

Interesting and informative methods of prodding the reluctant writer. The author discusses right-brain techniques in the teaching of the writing process. Excellent for use in any classroom.

Van Straalen, Alice, *The Book of Holidays Around the World* (New York, NY: E.P. Dutton, 1986).

Offers a variety of events for every day of the year. Beautifully illustrated.

INDEX

INDEX

INDEX

INDEX